INTENTION AND UNINTENTION OR THE HYPERCONSCIOUS IN CONTEMPORARY LYRIC IMPULSE

Grant Caldwell is a senior lecturer in the Creative Writing program at University of Melbourne. His latest books are the novel *Love and Derangement* (Arcadia, 2014), and *Reflections of a Temporary Self: New & Selected Poems* (Collective Effort/Trojan Press, 2015). He was awarded Australia Council for the Arts Established Writers Fellowships in 1992 and 1994. His research interests include the psychology of composition, the writing of poetry and fiction, concrete poetry and the origins and writing of haiku.

INTENTION AND UNINTENTION OR THE HYPERCONSCIOUS IN CONTEMPORARY LYRIC IMPULSE

Grant Caldwell

ARCADIA

First published 2018 by ARCADIA

the general books' imprint of

Australian Scholarly Publishing Pty Ltd

7 Lt Lothian St Nth, North Melbourne, Vic 3051

Tel: 03 9329 6963 / Fax: 03 9329 5452

enquiry@scholarly.info / www.scholarly.info

ISBN 978-1-925588-80-4

Cover design: Wayne Saunders
Cover graphic: Grant Caldwell

Where the unconscious was, consciousness shall go.

Jacques Lacan

CONTENTS

ACKNOWLEDGMENTS

The thesis that is the basis for this monograph was researched and written part time at Deakin University between 2006 and 2011, comprising the critical component which makes up this monograph, and a creative component, a collection of poetry, that was published by Five Island Press in 2010 as *glass clouds*. It only recently occurred to me to approach ASP with the manuscript and I am delighted that they agreed to publish it. Since the awarding of the doctorate in 2012 I have published two articles based on material taken from the thesis, in *New Scholar* and, in collaboration with Kevin Brophy, in *Text: Journal of writing and writing courses*. I would like to thank Professor David McCooey at Deakin University for his supervision of the project. Without David's help I am not sure I could have completed the thesis. I would also like to thank Deakin University and their administration staff for all of their willing and able help through the period of the candidature. Thanks too must go to Nick Walker, Helen Latemore, Anastasia Buryak and Wayne Saunders at Australian Scholarly Publishing, with special thanks to Nick Walker for publishing the book. Nick is a legend – or should be – in Australian publishing, often willing to take on difficult and unconventional projects, always with good humour, even when dealing with the unreasonable demands of some writers, such as myself. I would also like to thank my colleagues in the School of Culture and Communications at the University of Melbourne, especially those who were there while I was writing the thesis and working full time, and in particular those in the Creative Writing program at the time, Kevin

Brophy, Tony Birch, Amanda Johnson and Eddie Paterson. Their collegiality and support through those years while working full time was invaluable in completing the thesis. I would also like to send a special thanks to Angela O'Brien, who was Dean of the School of Creative Arts from 1995 to 2006, and who first opened the door for me to enter the university as a sessional teacher in 1995. Finally, I would like to thank my sister, Sue Caldwell for her support across the years, and my partner, Tang Yi, for all her support and encouragement over those six long years researching and writing the thesis.

The excerpted comments on the back of the book are taken from the thesis reports of two of the examiners, Paul Hetherington and Felicity Plunkett, to whom I also give my profound thanks.

INTRODUCTION: THE QUESTION OUTLINED AND THE KEY TERMS ADDRESSED: INTENTION, UNINTENTION AND HYPERCONSCIOUS

The objective of this dissertation is to make a fresh examination of the role of the unconscious drive in the impulse to write Western lyric poetry, in particular for contemporary lyric verse, in this age of quanta when meaning and certainty are deemed indeterminate. It will be argued that this unconscious drive is sourced through "unintention", during a poetic state, or what I will call "hyperconscious", that is driven by the poet's deep-rooted, subterranean personal forces, in concert with and subsequent to the "intention" or vocation or preparedness to write poems. For the purposes of this discourse, unintention is defined as the unselfconscious and spontaneous action of creation during a psychic state of hyperconsciousness. I am utilising the term "intention" here in a manner and context that I hope can be seen as once removed from the debate in literary theory. At one point in their essay "The Intentional Fallacy", William K. Wimsatt Jr. and Monroe C. Beardsley quote various inspirational anecdotes by writers, and then write: "All this, however, would appear to belong to an art separate from criticism, or to a discipline which one might call the psychology of composition ... different from the public science of evaluating poems" (1954, p. 9). In a later version of the essay they add: "The day may arrive when the psychology of composition is unified with the science of objective evaluation, but so far they are separate" (2001, p. 1380*).

Wimsatt and Beardsley make the key distinction between the science of objective analysis and the psychology of composition, and it is the latter that I will be examining in this thesis. The context of "intention" here is in relation to the motivating state or impulse to write, and not the meaning of the poem or the intention of the poet. I am concerned with intention as part of the psychological state of the poet at the time of the writing of the poem, especially in its first instance, but I will be arguing that "intention" is the state of mind in preparedness for or availability to the impulse. This may or may not be of use or interest to critics. I hope it will be of interest and use to creative writers and the teachers of creative writing.

Key to this examination is what I call the "poet-paradox": the notion that the self is not only what the lyric poet needs to discover and represent, but that it can be most vividly and truly represented only when the poet is not "present", during the peculiar focus of the hyperconscious; when the poet is least self-conscious. It will be useful to establish just what it is that lyric poetry is expressing, in general terms, and why it is that the difficulty or peculiarity of this expression generally necessitates hyperconsciousness. In this regard I will examine the poet and scholar C.K. Williams' work on what he calls the embodiment of emotion in poetry.

SCOPE

The scope of the dissertation will not allow for any in-depth examination of philosophical or neurological studies of consciousness and creativity.

* The original 1954 article does not include this sentence. It is added in the 2001 *Norton Anthology of Theory and Criticism* (see bibliography).

Nevertheless, some mention of David Rose, as well as T.S. Eliot's position on the "escape from personality" (1965, p. 29) will be made. Theodor Adorno questions the degree to which any psychological or philosophical position can be grasped: "Whoever chooses philosophy as a profession today must first reject the illusion that earlier philosophical enterprises began with: that the power of thought is sufficient to grasp the totality of the real" (1991–1992, p. 24). This limitation could equally be applied to psychoanalysis. Indeed, it will be suggested that even though the work of Freud (and Lacan) is helpful in understanding what *I am* talking about, it can in no way be claimed as axiomatic.

The above notwithstanding, it will still be useful at the outset to briefly examine the problems inherent in a philosophical notion of "consciousness" in order to further establish the general parameters of the study, if not to define exactly what they are. According to David Rose, the philosophical notion of "consciousness" is as problematic as the notion of "the mind". Rose points to "the most fundamental schism between whether 'the mind' comprises all thoughts that are potentially conscious, including memories and imaginings, or whether it also includes unconscious processes that can never become conscious" (2006, p. 4).

I therefore need to establish a guide to these key concepts of mind and consciousness, and whether they can be viewed as the same or separate entities, which I will do by examining Freud's studies on the subject of dreams. My thesis is that this study of the psychology of composition requires a very different approach to the matter of lyric verse than that taken by critical analysis: the latter is concerned with the investigation and interpretation of a literary work, whereas the psychology of composition, as I see it, is concerned with the investigation and description of the creative process and psychology of the poet, most particularly during the creative act. Accordingly, in order to address the psychology of composition I will investigate a small selection of individual poems and poets. I have chosen to focus on lyric poetry because the lyric poet is most likely to be writing from impulse, at least in the initial act, and because I take the position that most contemporary poetry is lyric in nature, or as David McCooey observes, "Lyricism is what we associate most commonly with poetry: musicality; brevity; intensity; the drive to epiphany or insight; and an emphasis on thought, feeling and subjectivity" (2005, p. 69).

In the discussion of the artistic psychological process, it will be presumed that the mind is the seat of consciousness, and that, rather than being limited to rational processes, it is seen as also encompassing all of that part of the psyche that is not conscious. It can therefore appear in some other form such as dreams and tropes: in other words, in all matter that human cognisance is capable of absorbing and storing, knowing and unknowing. Julia Kristeva's ideas on language and "the generating of significance" (2002, p. 27) could be seen to broaden this scope and to strengthen the argument. The dissertation will not enter into the argument as to where the mind (and hence consciousness) exists, except to note here that the Mandarin character for mind is "xin" 心 meaning literally "heart and mind". Suffice to say that it will be presumed that the expression (language) of psychological aspects of the artistic process (emotions and thoughts) come from the mind, or the psyche in all of its possible aspects, in its broadest possible sense. To map the psychological procedure of the lyric poet in composition from the perspective and psychology of the poet, it will be proposed that Western lyric poetry is the symptomatic outcome and manifestation of repressed or subterranean energies that in many ways parallel dream-wishes and states. As suggested already, this is not an examination of literary analysis or critical theory or literary theory but an attempt to argue from a fresh and more contemporary perspective that the lyric impulse to write poetry is essentially driven by the unconscious, where the psyche is altered and peculiar to the act. Central to the dissertation is the notion that this peculiar state of mind requires the poet to be minimally conscious of their self in the act, to the point that they are in an almost trance-like state, so that the self is unencumbered by its view of itself in the act of expression. This can then result in free manifestation of the unconscious in the work. The notions of intention and unintention will be central to the discourse, whereby there are three distinct but interlocking processes: a) Intention: education, vocation, availability; b) Unintention: impulse, idea, emanation, first draft; c) Review: editing, redrafting, completion. I will argue that the altered consciousness during the second stage, that is akin to some kind of poetic state (which I will call the hyperconscious), has changed somewhat today in comparison with the poetic state of the past, even from just fifty years ago.

In order to firmly locate the unconscious in the writing of lyric poetry, Freud's *The Interpretation of Dreams* (2004), will be examined in Chapter One, where a parallel will be made between the dream work and the poetry content or the matter that makes up the poem, indicating that the unconscious that drives the dream work has some equivalence in poetry, that the words "dream" and "poetry" can be exchanged in Freud's discourse on dreams. In Chapter Two, I will investigate Lacan's elaboration on Freud's elements of dreams in his essay "The Instance of the Letter in the Unconscious or Reason since Freud" (2004), and how Lacan indicates in depth the manner in which the unconscious might be seen to be working in the writing of lyric poems. C. K. Williams' notion of the embodiment of emotions in poetry (1998, p. 4) will be examined and applied in Chapter Three, in order to investigate just what it is that the unconscious of the lyric poet needs to express; how this necessitates the accessing of what Keats (1952), via Hazlitt, called Negative Capability, which determines and identifies the existence of the hyperconscious. This will also be shown as not inconsistent with T.S. Eliot's notion of the need for the poet to escape personality (1965, p. 29), and Williams' point that the need for embodiment of emotion is even more greater in today's age of quanta, when everything is uncertain and indeterminate. At this stage of the thesis, in Chapter Four, it will be important to study some concrete evidence of the hyperconscious state and its accessing of the unconscious. I will make case studies of two poems written by two contemporary Australian poets, Myron Lysenko (1998) and Ian McBryde (2001), demonstrating that at the time of composition, and even subsequent to publication of these poems, the poets were not aware of what were the true drivers of the poems. Through personal knowledge and informal interview with these poets I will reveal their subsequent acknowledgment of what I had perceived as the true underlying drivers of their poems. These poems are of course a small sample, but what they can be said to indicate is the possibility of the unconscious as the major driver of a lyric poem. I will argue that this is the case because during hyperconsciousness the poet is least inhibited, that they are least likely aware of, or concerned about, the fundamental inferences of what they are saying, and hence more able and likely to freely and tellingly express these inferences. The introduction of the term hyperconsciousness for the poetic state has been necessary in order to differentiate it from any previous awkward and misleading terms such as "the psychology of composition", or "trance-like state", or "day-dream", or "poetic state", to instead suggest a more compact, yet flexible and all-encompassing signifier that incorporates not only the psychoanalytical states of consciousness and unconsciousness, but which may indicate multi-states, in a unique, perhaps dynamic manner, when the poet is peculiarly focused. The term "inspired" or "inspiration", while useful, has become vague with use and variation of application, and may not even be applicable in the modern and postmodern context. As Timothy Clark points out in his book, *The Theory of Inspiration*: "The discourse of inspiration has often comprised a tight knot of different, even contradictory, claims about subjectivity, value and productivity" (1997, p. 3). Clark also points out that the word "inspire" comes from the Latin "to breathe or blow into" which implies that it comes from without, and is thus more akin to the myth of the descending muse prevalent in previous times. I want to herein differentiate the contemporary lyric impulse from that of inspiration. To this end I will use the terms "emanation" or "impulse" where it is necessary. Given the various reports on the poetic state by poets over the years, I think it is reasonable to say that the hyperconscious is various and variant in its manifestation between artists, as well as varying for individual artists at different times, and that it incorporates a multiplicity of psychic degrees of intensity, known and knowable. Clark investigates this question of agency at length in his first chapter. I would like to employ his statement as a given for this entire discourse, that: "no psychological state in itself guarantees the worth of its products to others" (1997, p. 16). In other words, the process I am describing and its inherent psychological determinants are not meant to necessarily suggest a resultant lyric verse of any quality: they are a description of the process and what I see as the major drive, and the connected paradox of the absent self in the impulse to compose lyric verse.

HYPERCONSCIOUS, INTENTION AND UNINTENTION

Of the three stages of the lyric process that I have briefly outlined already: intention, unintention and review, it is the second stage, which is the attitude of the hyperconscious, that requires most attention, and for this reason I will here closely examine the term. For all its apparent complexity, the hyperconscious might be definable in general terms. In its more prosaic sense the term alludes to the psychic state of the lyric poet in the period of response to their unintentional impulse: that is to say, the lyric poet's period of greatest creative intensity exists when they are least inhibited, most unselfconscious, and not (or minimally) conscious of "themselves". But just what I mean by "greatest creative intensity", and how and why it occurs in this state I hope to investigate and argue in the body of the dissertation.

The question of automatic writing may arise here, as it does for Clark, as a means to this unintentional state. I want to make a clear distinction between what I am calling the hyperconscious impulse and any writing "method", such as the Automatic Writing of the surrealists. What I am alluding to is not procedural or methodological, it is an unpredictable and spontaneous state that is nevertheless anticipated through a conscious preparation of availability or intention to at some stage experience the impulse necessitating and creating such a state. I am not dismissing the possibility of writing powerful lyric poetry by some procedure such as automatic writing or individual ritual, but I am not concerned with such procedures. What I am arguing here is that the unintentional action is more likely to reach more profoundly and intensely the unconscious vault of thoughts and feelings, precisely because it is then that the conscious self is truly least involved. Clark writes that: "the surrealist movement was the fullest attempt to realize a programme of calculated inspiration" (1997, p. 195). I am not talking here of any *programme of calculated inspiration*, as I see this as a contradiction in terms, especially if I am to apply it to my notion of the poetic state being an emanation rather than an inspiration. There is no calculation or intention in the impulse to write lyric poetry that I am examining: the only intention exists before the writing action, in the education and preparedness and availability to write. Clark's examination of the surrealist experiments constantly refers to *programmes, modelling,* and *strenuous conditions* (1997, p. 197), suggesting the opposite of what I am alluding to. What Clark and Breton (and Paul Valéry before them, with "La Juene Parque" (1953)), describe is a conflation of my intention and unintention, whereas I see these two as mutually exclusive: the intention is the vocation; the unintention is the expected but not predictable action.

INTENTION

I have indicated that I want to focus on the period of unintentional creation, but an understanding of the other stages of the process I am suggesting is contextually important, especially for the term intention, as it is here that my process differs greatly from others, such as Paul Valéry. The term intention here refers to the education (in its broadest sense), preparedness, and vocational attitude of the poet, whether young or old, inexperienced or experienced: the *attitude* of being available to the act, intending to *at some time* write poetry, whether immediately, imminently or in the vague future of days. Ted Berrigan called this *attitude*, "always on" (1997, p. 53). In his address to a creative writing group, his talk later anthologised as "Incredible Masterpieces", he claims:

> being a poet is a twenty-four-hour-a-day-thing. You're always on … What Allen [Ginsberg] refers to as mindfulness is simply that. It's a matter of being awake, alive, alert, aware of possibilities. If you're a poet, all of that is partly channelled into the fact that maybe you're going to write some of them down, too. (Berrigan, 1997, p. 53)

Apart from this vocational intention, there is no consistent, uniform "means" to this unintentional hyperconscious state of creative impulse, and nor is there an identifiable, proven source. Even the use of drugs, which I do not have room or scope to address adequately here, cannot be argued as a proven avenue, although many poets and artists have been known to develop addictions that parallel their creative drives.

This dissertation is not concerned with the source or otherwise of the hyperconscious, rather with its existence and the question of intentionality or otherwise. The argument is that the only clear, identifiable intention of the lyric poet is to write poetry *at some stage* and that the subject matter, moment of impulse or "epiphany" to write is not predictable. If it is predictable, the poet is not completely (if at all) cognisant or "conscious" of all of the implications of, or reasons for, choosing the substance or language of the poem; they are in that state the least aware of the true drivers of the poem. In the third stage, that of review and revision they may become aware of the drives and implications as by this stage the deeper unconscious impulse may have been exposed.

Thomas De Quincey (1961) quotes Wordsworth on the prerequisites for epiphany that may suggest these notions of intention and unintention. Late one night, Wordsworth had been lying prostrate on a country road listening for the horse and wagon delivering the London newspapers from Robert Southey, who had had them before him – apparently they were passed around among these poets and writers thus – when he stood up and reflecting a moment, said:

> if, under any circumstances, the attention is energetically braced up to an act of steady observation or of steady expectation, then, if this intense condition of vigilance should suddenly relax, at that moment any beautiful, any impressive visual object, or collection of objects, falling upon the eye, is carried to the heart with a power not known under other circumstances. (De Quincey, 1997, p. 122)

The key phrase here is, for our purposes: "braced up to an act of steady observation or of steady expectation, and this intense condition of vigilance", which could be a description of my idea of intention. However, I prefer to expand this notion to both the general and the specific education of the poet in the broadest sense of the term education. Wordsworth's idea of the momentary relaxation of attention resulting in epiphany could be seen as the moment of unselfconscious, hyperconscious impulse when an object or situation or even an idea or memory, brings about this "relaxed" mode, when the self, or self-consciousness, is no longer dominant, enabling the psyche to freely express itself. At another time Wordsworth described this as "whatever suspends the comparing powers of the mind" (1974, p. 353). It is this "comparing powers of the mind" that I warrant chiefly inhibits the poet-self, for it is without this suspension that the poet is unable to transcend the perceived self and, as a result cannot freely express themselves. For surely all comparison in the mind is based upon the self and the situation of the self. This is key to my argument as it suggests the necessity of the loss of self-consciousness. Otherwise we are delivered "an art in which the poet, retaining control, risks nothing" (Clark, paraphrasing Breton, p. 200). The truly lyric poet risks everything, as they write, in that second stage of unintention, without conscious control: unselfconsciously, unconsciously, revealing not only more than they intend, but also more than they realise.

What I am suggesting is that the lyric poet needs to be available to (intention) an unpredictable unselfconscious poetic state (unintention: hyperconsciousness), so that they can inhabit the "absolute presence" of timeless illumination when, to more or lesser degree, they are completely in the present moment, when even the term "immediate" is not sufficiently "present"; when the sense of the self is "absent". Of course, this immediately suggests a paradox: that in order for the poet to have absolute presence, they must be psychologically absent – that is, not conscious of themselves. I have no trouble with this apparent paradox: it reflects the paradoxical nature of what I am attempting to illuminate. I only hope that, in accepting the paradox, a clearer understanding can be established. This paradox will be explored in the final chapter.

It is the contention of this dissertation that the poet is at all times intentional, except when during the hyperconscious state of the creative impulse, but that this vigilance, what Robert Langbaum calls "the sensitized condition of the observer" (1978, p. 37), is not always conscious or self-conscious. That is to say the poet is not necessarily in a constant state of "being a poet", but through practice and habit they are always in a state of availability to it, whether this is triggered or not, or acted upon or not.

CHAPTER ONE

SOURCING THE UNCONSCIOUS IN THE HYPERCONSCIOUS: FREUD'S *THE INTERPRETATION OF DREAMS* AND THE PROCESS OF INTENTION AND UNINTENTION

In reading Freud's "The Interpretation of Dreams" (2004), it becomes evident that there are possible parallels between Freud's *dream-content* and the content of lyric poems: both are arguably, more or less, an expression of the unconscious. However, where the dream content takes the form of images, later "transcribed" by the dreamer or patient into verbal language and later still by the psychoanalyst into a formal written language as dream thoughts representing what the dreamer remembers, the content of a lyric poem is most often expressed, at least in the initial draft (at the time of the hyperconscious impulse), in a *written language* that is *the language of poetry.* Of course sometimes this language of poetry is, like dream thoughts, employed at a distance from the inspired moment, "recollected in tranquillity" as

Wordsworth put it (1986, p. 151). I would make the point that, for lyric poetry, this delayed action is, or is akin to, a secondary process of creative composition, and what I have identified as the third stage in the lyric process. I will explain these three stages below, but I need to point out that what I am mostly interested in pursuing in this discourse is the second stage, the impulse that the poet acts upon, even if it does turn out to be a first draft of a later finished poem, as seems most commonly the case.

When I write of the language of poetry, I am referring to what Paul Valéry called "poetic language" (1958, p. 171), or what Victor Shklovsky identified as "defamiliarization" or "making strange" (1965, p. 12). Valéry suggested a distinction between "general language" and "poetic language". He defined the task of the former as: "fulfilled when each sentence has been completely abolished, annulled, and replaced by the meaning" (1958, p. 171). In other words, this language is so commonly used that the meaning that most people will so readily perceive and know makes them unconcerned and unconscious of it as language and what makes up that language. On the other hand, Valéry saw poetic language as "dominated by *personal* conditions: by conscious, continuous, and sustained musical feeling ... another quite distinct system" (1958, p. 171). That is, poetic language is subjective and emotional. Shklovsky made the same distinction between "practical language and poetic language" (1965, p. 10) in 1917 when he argued that the essential purpose of art is to overcome the deadening effects of habit by representing things in unfamiliar ways: "to impart the sensation of things as they are perceived and not as they are known" (1965, p. 12). This was the basis of his Formalist theory of Defamiliarization (this word is a translation of the anglicised Russian *ostranenie*; literally, "making strange"). Further on in his essay Shklovsky says:

> After we see an object several times, we begin to recognize it. The object is in front of us and we know about it, but we do not see it

> – hence we cannot say anything significant about it. Art removes objects from the automatism of perception. (1965, p. 13)

Hence poetic language becomes an individual choice, a personal rather than a common device that evolves from the intentional (and continual) learning and practice that allows its expert development and manipulation, so that, for the poet, the images and feelings are expressed as they appear, as if seen or felt for the first time, with the automatism of perception removed. Shklovsky expresses it thus:

> And now, today, when the artist wishes to deal with living form and with the living, not the dead, word, and wishes to give the word features, he has broken it down and mangled it up … New, living words are created. The ancient diamonds of words recover their former brilliance. This new language is incomprehensible, difficult, and cannot be read like the *Stock Exchange Bulletin*. (1973, p. 46)

Of course, this mangling of words into diamonds, this application of poetic language is not necessarily confined to the second stage of unintention; it can occur during the third stage of review. However, I would argue that the degree of the poetic language is greater during hyperconsciousness, because the poet is drawing less self-consciously on their language. The result is that the language is more "defamiliarized" because the poet is less inhibited in applying it.

As a poet, Valéry was aware of this subliminal drive. He recognised the hidden origins of impulse that are expressed in the poetic language of lyric verse:

> discourses which make up verse, which are so bizarrely ordered, which don't correspond to any need, if not the need that they must create themselves; which always only speak of absent things or of the things which are profoundly and secretly experienced; strange

> discourses which seem crafted by another person than the one who said them, and to address themselves to another person than the one who is hearing them. In sum, it's a language within a language. (1957, p. 1324)

The "absent things or the things which are profoundly and secretly experienced" reflects what I am proposing as the unconscious drive, when the poet is in what Valéry calls "the poetic state" of "exalted inspiration" (Ince, 1961, pp. 112–14)*. Here I will repeat the point made in the introductory chapter, that the term inspiration is no longer so apt, now that the external demons and muses have become inner psychology and impulse. If Valéry were writing today he may well use the term "exalted impulse" or "exalted emanation".

Valéry's model for the stages in the poetic experience have been depicted by W.N. Ince in his study *The Poetic Theory of Paul Valéry (Inspiration and Technique)* (1961) as: I Preparation, II Illumination, III Composition, with a further division, that of "intimation", occurring between the second and third stages. I see a clear parallel between Valéry's "Preparation" and my notion of intention. But before I go into this I should outline what I understand as the lyric process and how it coincides with and diverges from Valéry. Ince also states that Valéry is never clear if he is talking of his own experience as a poet or if he is speaking for poets in general. Accordingly, I feel I should explain that my idea of the process is intended to apply to lyric poets in general. It is, however, based mostly on my own experience. I see the process as a series of stages: I Intention (education, reading, vocation, preparedness); II Illumination (hyperconscious emanation and impulse to compose unintentionally); III Review and reworking†.

* I am using the translation and interpretation of Valéry's work by W.N. Ince (1961).

† There are rare occasions when this third stage is not necessary, when the poem comes fully formed in stage two.

According to Ince, Valéry's first stage "is essentially one of reflection and analysis, and not least, self-analysis ... a patient, determined search for precise formulations in the field of knowledge and self-knowledge" (Ince, 1961, p. 96). What aligns this stage even more closely to my idea of "intention" is the later statement by Ince that Valéry "stresses, however, that such researches are most valuable when they have been pursued for their intrinsic worth with no regard for practical consequences" (Ince, 1961, p. 97). For me, as for Valéry, the period of intentional "learning" generally has as its object the art and history of poetry, which for me would include the reading of verse. It would even include the imminent production of verse, but not the actual writing of it. It should be added, somewhat contradictorily, that the writing and re-writing of verse in stages two and three adds to and is part of the first stage of education and preparedness. As has been explained previously, intention is defined as a vocational attitude, an intention to be a (lyric) poet, to thus immerse oneself in the art and history of poetry, and to be available to the impulses that will trigger the writing of it, which one will do, when the impulse comes, *unintentionally*.

The connection to and the distinction between my ideas and those of Valéry are made more apparent when we consider that he wrote his long work "La Jeune Parque" (The Youngest Fate) from "a painstaking attempt to reproduce faithfully the structure and mechanisms of dreams according to his scientific understanding of their nature" (Lewis, 1976, p. 459). In their essay in *Psychoanalytical Review*, Dorothy Otnow Lewis and Melvin Lewis examine how Valéry applied the same or similar structural elements of dreams as articulated by Freud to his poem, "La Jeune Parque" (Lewis, 1976). The difference between what Valéry did (and what the Lewises are describing), and what I am attempting to explain here, is that Valéry "could still (only) honestly describe 'La Jeune Parque' as an 'exercise'" (Ince, 1961, p. 97); and that he and the Lewises are therefore applying Freud's ideas of dreams to a poem written with the *plan* of paralleling the structural elements of a dream; whereas I am using these dream elements to suggest the same or similar unconscious (*unintentional*) mechanisms in the writing of lyric verse.

Valéry's understanding of the first stage of Preparation, as "essentially one of reflection and analysis, and, not least, self-analysis" (Ince, 1961, p. 96), reinforces my notion of intention. Valéry's term Preparation suggests planning or too strong a sense of control over the timing or occurrence of the impulse to write, the second stage. This period that I call intention is, for me, a long-term period of continuing vocational preparedness, leading to availability to the impulse. It is educational as well as reflective, and Valéry too sees that "[t]he poet can acquire sound notions about the nature of language and its particular form in literature and poetry" (Ince, 1961, p. 98).

When Valéry writes that "[t]o know oneself really well is ... to be on the threshold of original creation" (Ince, 1961, p. 99), he reflects the poet-paradox already alluded to, where, although the poet writes from a position of self-knowledge, he or she writes "strange discourses which seem crafted by another person" (Ince, 1961, p. 99). This point is central to this dissertation: that hyperconsciousness is a poetic state wherein the greatest illumination of the self is possible only because the poet is in such an unselfconscious state. I am aware that Valéry is not exactly saying this, but I am using his ideas to support the notion that this unselfconscious, hyperconscious state is essential for the unintentional attitude, when the poet is so deeply absorbed in the impulse to create the initial draft of the poem, when they are not thinking about who they are or how they appear to others, when their inhibitions are minimised. In her lecture to students at the University of Melbourne on 22 March 2011, Melbourne poet Claire Gaskin said:

> When I remove myself from the poem and let it be what it wants to be, not what I want it to be, it is a stronger poem and ironically this makes it more of myself not less of myself and more self-revealing.

Where Valéry separates *illumination* and *composition*, I see composition and illumination occurring concurrently, even if the subsequent work of review and reworking on the first drafts of the poem takes weeks, months, even years of review and careful re-composition. And no matter how much the form and language of the poem changes in this time, it retains the initial underlying impulse that first triggered it.

Kenneth Koch makes reference to the three stages I have been discussing, specifically for lyric verse, in his book, *The Art of Poetry (Poems, Parodies, Interviews, Essays, and Other work)* from 1996:

> *To write only lyrics is to be sad, perhaps,*
> *Or fidgety, or overexcited, too dependent on circumstance –*
> *But there is a way out of that. The lyric must be bent*
> *Into a more operative form, so that*
> *Fragments of being reflect absolutes (see for example the verse of*
> *William Carlos Williams or Frank O'Hara), and you can go on*
> *Without saying it all every time. If you can master the knack of it,*
> *You are a fortunate poet, and a skilled one. You should read*
> *A great deal, and be thinking of writing poetry all the time.*
> *Total absorption in poetry is one of the finest things in existence –*
> *It should not make you feel guilty. Everyone is absorbed in something.*
> *The sailor is absorbed in the sea. Poetry is the meditation of life.*
> (Koch, 1996, p. 13)

In this excerpt, Koch's outline, while presented in a different order, nevertheless allows a reiteration of what I am arguing: my second stage, Illumination to Impulse, he expresses as: "To write only lyrics is to be sad, perhaps, / Or fidgety, or overexcited, too dependent on circumstance". This edginess is symptomatic of the need or impulse to write, the symptom of the unconscious drive prompting the need to express the personal. My third stage, Review, Koch's words describe as: "The lyric must be bent / Into a more operative form, so that / Fragments of being reflect absolutes". This describes the process when the poet is more self-conscious and can perceive the absolutes that are suggested in the preliminary work, and when the language can be made more acute. At this stage the poet may still not be aware of the unconscious personal drives in the initial impulse, but they will be aware of the weaknesses or inappropriateness of structure or language that need addressing, even if only by instinct. My first stage of intention, Koch describes as: "You should read / A great deal, and be thinking of writing poetry all the time. / Total absorption in poetry is one of the finest things in / existence –". Here is the poet's education and preparedness for the writing, whenever the impulse occurs: to be "thinking of writing poetry all the time" does not mean that the poet does write all the time, but that they are available to it.

SPONTANEITY

Any discussions around intentional attitude, or availability, leading to the unintentional response to the lyric impulse should include an examination of the question of spontaneity, or what Monet called "instantaneity". In his book *Creativity*, Kevin Brophy addresses the binary or "oppositions" of spontaneity and planning: "to see again how one of these terms has been suppressed in the promotion of a certain image and value connected with creativity" (1998, pp. 12–13). Brophy is referring to spontaneity as the promoted term, and while I am mostly concerned with that area of the creative process, because it is the least identifiable, I also acknowledge the importance or significance of "planning" in the process. However, I am making the distinction between what I am calling "intention" and what Brophy is referring to as "planning". I see planning as more project specific, whereas preparedness is vocationally general. Brophy uses Monet to illustrate his point of concern regarding the justification for the dominance of the term "spontaneity" in "the rise of the avant-garde, and its earliest art movement, Impressionism, [which] is named for the quality of spontaneous 'impressions' in the paintings of this period" (1998, p. 13). Brophy writes that Monet named his technique "instantaneity" when in fact it was not really any such thing: Monet's work "was accomplished in a painstaking manner which resulted in a painted surface that gave the impression of spontaneous brushstrokes" (Brophy, 1998, p. 13). This is perhaps a warranted questioning of Monet's sincerity, but it does not refute the possibility of spontaneity in Impressionism or the Impressionists as a whole. Brophy's point seems to be based on the presumption that spontaneity cannot be connected with any kind of "planning". This seems fair enough at first thought. But he is not suggesting that it cannot involve "preparedness to write". I am saying that these two things, "planning" and "preparedness to write" are very different things. The lyric poet can of course plan to write, but I am arguing that a) it is the general preparedness for the spontaneous impulse to write that mostly unearths the lyric self that is driven by the unconscious, and b) even if a poem *is* planned, or mapped out in advance, there are still subterranean forces, unconscious drives that are informing whatever is written. Brophy actually illustrates this general distinction himself when he describes Jack Kerouac's process in writing *On the Road*:

> Signs of spontaneity give Jack Kerouac's quintessential beat novel, *On the Road*, its particular sheen and its particular place as a work of modern prose. Kerouac took three weeks to write the novel in 1950, but then it was seven years in the rewriting. (1998, p. 14)

Here is a succinct and lucid description of the second and third stages of my model: the second stage, the hyperconscious three weeks, when Kerouac wrote, one might imagine, in a series of spontaneous, unselfconscious periods; and the third, review stage: the considered, more self-conscious, less spontaneous, rewriting and editing period of seven years.

FREUD'S *THE INTERPRETATION OF DREAMS* AND THE UNCONSCIOUS IN THE POEM

Freud uses the dream-content of the dreamer's recall and "translates" or writes his interpretation of it, interpreting what he sees as the broader implications and symbolic references of the content. Although this act of writing follows the relating/remembering by the dreamer, these dream thoughts of Freud and other psychoanalysts speculate on what has prompted or engendered (preceded) the dream. In the case of the poet, the act of writing or "translating" occurs almost immediately upon the impulse to write, although this can sometimes be "recollected in tranquillity" (Wordsworth, 1986, p. 151). Both the psychoanalyst and the poet require a kind of interpretation and translation and I am arguing that they are both accessing the unconscious. The difference is that the psychoanalyst is accessing the unconscious of the dreamer, whereas the poet is accessing her or his own unconscious, and has intended or prepared to be available to the impulse to do so (write) at some indeterminate stage. When this impulse does occur, the poet engages the hyperconscious, whereby the sense of self is minimised or else objectified as another.

I suggest that it is the poet's and the artist's normal state to be isolated in some way, physically and/or psychologically, if not more than non-artists, then with more of a preparedness to express this isolation: more of a need, a habit, a learned ability, which leads to them being more "fidgety, or overexcited, too dependent on circumstance –", as Koch puts it (1996, p. 13). In this way the poet can both observe and experience the society or phenomenon that is being meditated upon with less interference, not so much (or only) from others, but from themselves in relation to others, from their idea of themselves, or, in Freud's terms, from their ego, their consciousness. This isolation is not always obvious in its manifestation, and is sometimes subtle, but it is necessary in some form so that the poet is available to the impulse and the subsequent engagement of the hyperconscious. In this way the poet can be more truly able to demonstrate "For *I* is someone else" (Rimbaud, 1966, p. 305).*

This idea that in order to write the lyric poet needs to reduce their self-consciousness, or their sense of who they are, accords somewhat with T.S. Eliot's notions on the personality of the poet:

> It [the business of a poet] is a concentration, and a new thing resulting from the concentration, of a very great number of experiences ... [Poetry] is not the expression of personality, but an escape from personality. (1965, p. 29)

For in this isolation, the poet is able to achieve this concentration, so that they may be impersonal in their concentration. This reflects well a major point of this dissertation: that in this impersonality, the poet's unconscious (hidden, buried, repressed) psyche comes into play. And it is in this state, again, as I will expand on in Chapter Five, that the poet is most likely to *be*, to reflect him or her self: the poet-paradox of the sense of self as absent in order to be truly present.

In one of his almost daily letters to his fiancée, Felice, whom he met with just five times in the five years of their engagement, Kafka wrote:

> writing means revealing oneself to excess ... This is why one can never be alone enough when one writes, why there can never be enough silence around when one writes, why even night is not night enough. (1992, pp. 183–4)

In order to reveal "oneself to excess" the poet cannot be "present": their ego cannot be present, or it will get in the way of "revealing [themselves] to excess"; it will block the truer, deeper ideas and feelings of their unconscious. In many

* Usually translated these days as "For *I* is another". For my purposes, I prefer the original translation, as it seems to infer a more definite "someone else".

ways, Eliot supports this, when he writes: "The emotion of art is impersonal. And the poet cannot reach this impersonality without surrendering himself wholly to the work to be done" (Eliot, 1965, p. 30). Eliot also writes that: "this is not quite the whole story. There is a great deal, in the writing of poetry, which must be conscious and deliberate" (Eliot, 1965, p. 29). Here it seems he is referring to what I see as the third stage of the process of composition: the review and reworking of the raw material that has come from the impulse to unintentional work. But equally Eliot could be noting that even in these highly focused states, the poet's consciousness is not entirely absent: it is still present and able to direct what is written to some extent. In other words, the conscious ego may not always be as absent as I am suggesting. Here the distinction between the hyperconscious and the unconscious is evident: the former may source the unconscious, but not exclusively. Equally, in the third stage of the review, it is reasonable to assume that the hyperconscious may be engaged to some degree in the redrafting of the work.

To return to Freud, and to summarise: the act of expression for the dreamer is the dream (the dream content in images), and it is the psychoanalyst who interprets the dream content, writing it up as the dream thoughts. On the other hand the act of expression for the poet is the poem (an interpretation or expression of the poet's thoughts, images and feelings in poetic language). How then can a perceived nexus between dream and poetry be useful to this dissertation?

In his *The Interpretation of Dreams*, Freud makes the point that he and other psychoanalysts have introduced what he calls "dream thoughts", namely, the "latent content" of the dreams, sourced through the understanding and interpretation of their manifest content (2004, p. 400). If we replace the word "dream" with the word "poetry" in this statement, the inherent ideas can be seen to be equally relevant for the textual analysis of poetry: the analysis of a text that is expressing thoughts and feeling indirectly. As

I have pointed out already, in dream-thoughts, language is interpreting or "translating" the dreamer's memory of images or signs, whereas in the analysis of poetry, language is interpreting language, albeit "poetic" language. But this dissertation is concerned with the original impulse or source of the lyric poem, not the analysis, interpretation or "translation" of its manifest content, even if this will sometimes require working backwards, from the content of the poem to its possible source. And so, in order not to confuse my objectives, I will continue to pursue an understanding of the source of the impulse.

Looking in more detail at Freud's work on the process of dream formation, it is even more evident that he could just as easily be referring to the process of artistic composition. This is clearer if we ensure we are looking at it from the perspective of the psychology of composition and not the critical or textual analysis of literature. If we do this, Freud provides us with language for and insight into that process. There are some obvious but important distinctions between what we might call the dream-psyche and the composition-psyche: in composition the conscious is more or less engaged, even to the extent that it is providing substance and/or some kind of structure (at least more structure than in the dream-psyche). Also, the hyperconscious is expressed in written language, whereas the dream content is made up of non-linguistic images. And finally, the poem usually includes signs and images that the poet is more or less controlling, through language, whereas the dreamer rarely *seems* to be in control of his or her dream (although there are reported instances where some element of control is exerted by dreamers).

In suggesting through Freud a similarity (if not a correlation) between the impulse for the poem and the origin of the dream, the question of composition may be brought closer to general understanding. But further questions arise: what is the state of mind of the poet when composing? What has led to this state of mind? How close or similar is it to the mind of the dreamer, and can a consideration of this question be of any use?

In *The Interpretation of Dreams*, Freud uses a rebus to demonstrate the distinction between dream-content and dream-thoughts, explaining:

> we can only form a proper judgement of the rebus if we ... try to replace each separate element by a syllable or word that can be represented by that element in some way or other. The words which are put together in this way are no longer nonsensical but may form a poetical phrase of the greatest beauty and significance. (2004, pp. 400–1)

In other words, Freud's interpretation of the dream content in writing up the dream thoughts is, in effect, a similar process to that of the poet writing the poem: the dream-thoughts, *and* the poet, are "interpreting"* or expressing (for the poet) what the unconscious has "thrown up", and the result (in both cases) "may form a poetical phrase of the greatest beauty and significance" (Freud, 2004, p. 401). This clearly establishes a parallel link between the dream thoughts and the unconscious source of the poem. If we can accept Freud's establishment of the unconscious as the source of the dream-thoughts, it is reasonable to accept that the source of poetry, lyric poetry in particular, is the unconscious, at least to a considerable degree. Note that this applies to the source of the lyric impulse, just as the dream-thoughts are the speculated source of the dream-impulse or its latent content. What that unconscious is, exactly, remains unclear, and the extent of its role in the lyric impulse is also uncertain, but what I am suggesting in this discourse is that it is the major driver of the lyric poem.

By interpreting the dream-content and writing up the dream thoughts, Freud is paralleling, albeit in a non-poetic, more scientific manner, the process by which the poet expresses their unconscious thoughts and emotions (if more or less unconsciously), in words/language. And this is precisely where the "art" of the poet becomes paramount: the need to

* I am using Freud's term here for the action of the psychoanalyst.

describe, express, evoke with their primary tool, language. In their reading and practice the poet refines their linguistic and symbolic and structural adeptness until these become somewhat natural, so that they can then more easily slip into the hyperconscious stage. Les Murray's exuberant rendition of what I am calling hyperconsciousness is typical of poets' articulations of their experiences:

> It's wonderful, there's nothing else like it, you write in a trance. And the trance is completely addictive, you love it, you want more of it. Once you've written the poem and had the trance, polished it and so on, you can go back to the poem and have a trace of that trance, have the shadow of it, but you can't have it fully again. It seemed to be a knack I discovered as I went along. It's an integration of the body-mind and the dreaming-mind and the daylight-conscious-mind. All three are firing at once, they're all in concert. You can be sitting there but inwardly dancing, and the breath and the weight and everything else are involved, you're fully alive. It takes a while to get into it. You have to have some key, like say a phrase or a few phrases or a subject matter or maybe even a tune to get you started going towards it, and it starts to accumulate. Sometimes it starts without your knowing that you're getting there, and it builds in your mind like a pressure. I once described it as being like a painless headache, and you know there's a poem in there, but you have to wait until the words form. (1998, no p.n.)

In Murray's words, the hyperconscious is the "concert" of the unconscious and the conscious, becoming a habit that comes upon the poet as a trance: this is the transition from the intention (preparedness) to the unintention (action) for the poet. But the power of the trance depends on the self as absent, when the self is so absorbed in a subject, even if that subject is the self. In this state they are no longer conscious of themselves, so that the "mind" in all its forms can "inwardly dance" unselfconsciously. I will expand on this idea in Chapter Five.

Of course, as Murray suggests, it is later, when the poet reflects on these "notes" written while "asleep" in the trance, that they have a chance to judge, to understand, to reshape and edit this raw material come from the "dream". And it is in this stage of reshaping that the poet somewhat resembles the psychoanalyst interpreting the dream: the poet, in reshaping and reworking the raw poem is often interpreting what the hyperconscious has uncovered, so as to best present (or best hide, or make less obvious) what has been recognised.

In extending this premise of the dream/poetry nexus, Freud's discussion of the three essential elements of dream-content interpreted in dream-thoughts: condensation, displacement and overdetermination, might be seen to reflect similar elements for the composition of lyric verse. In this way the existence, if not the predominance, of the unconscious in lyric composition might be more extensively established. As has been suggested above, I am here speaking of the initial draft work – the second Illumination/composition stage – and not the third stage of Review/reworking of the poem.

Freud identified *condensation* as one of the most obvious elements of dream-content, when compared to dream-thoughts. By condensation, Freud means compression of subject matter in dreams, so that the "analysis setting out the dream-thoughts underlying it may occupy six, eight or a dozen times as much space" than the dream-content, and even then, if the interpretation is carried further "it may reveal still more thoughts concealed behind the dream" (2004, p. 401). Indeed, Freud concludes that: "Strictly speaking, then, it is impossible to determine the amount of condensation". If we make a parallel with the writing of poetry in what I am calling the hyperconscious state, it might be seen that here too it is impossible to determine the amount of condensation, or what the inferences and underlying meanings are for the lyric poet. Freud describes the condensation in dreams as "brief, meagre and laconic in comparison with the range and wealth of the dream-thoughts"

(2004, p. 401), and in doing so he could easily be describing the succinctness, the concentrated suggestion of poems. Further on, he writes, "It must not be forgotten, however, that we are dealing with an *unconscious* process of thought, which may easily be different from what we perceive during purposive reflection accompanied by consciousness" (2004, p. 402). Again, this observation could be a description of the second and third stages of the process I am suggesting, from the *unconscious* lyric impulse to the *reflective* review and reworking of the first draft.

Freud explains *overdetermination* as follows: "Not only are the elements of a dream determined by the dream-thoughts many times over, but the individual dream-thoughts are represented in the dream by several elements" (2004, p. 404). This kind of overdetermination or, over-representation, is also evident in the poem, directly and through imagery, as the dominant, overriding or central metaphor or image or idea of the poem. In Myron Lysenko's poem* it is the idea of the brother being stuck, and the poet's feeling of helplessness at the time, conveyed (overdetermined) by repeated lines and phrases: "he couldn't / move up, / he couldn't / move down" (1998, p. 43) (twice); "I couldn't / find him", "couldn't / see him", "stuck / halfway" (twice), "stuck there", "I didn't know what to do", "suspended" (p. 43). While in Ian McBryde's poem it is the abandoned, helpless sailors, lost in the vast amorphous sea that is predominate in words and phrases such as "water" (five times), "under the surface" (p. 23), "the water is/softening me" (p. 24); "the ocean is choking me" (p. 24); "just / keep him from sinking" (p. 25).

Freud could easily be describing the process of constructing a poem as he goes on to say that:

> a dream is constructed, rather, by a whole mass of dream-thoughts being submitted to a sort of manipulative process in which those

* Lysenko's complete poem appears at the start of Chapter 4, and McBryde's poem appears in the Appendix.

elements which have the most numerous and strongest supports acquire the right entry into the dream-content. (2004, p. 404)

His third essential element of dream-thoughts, *Displacement*, presented Freud with some difficulty, as it seemed to suggest a somewhat opposing function to *overdetermination*. In outlining *displacement*, Freud states:

> It could be seen that the elements which stand out as the principle components of the manifest content of the dream are far from playing the same part in the dream-thoughts. And, as a corollary, the converse of this assertion can be affirmed: what is clearly the essence of the dream-thoughts need not be represented in the dream at all. The dream is, as it were, differently centred from the dream-thoughts – its content has different elements as its central point. (2004, p. 410)

Of course, for the purposes of this dissertation, we are not wholly concerned with Freud's difficulty, except in its relation to what can be seen as making a parallel with the composition of lyric poetry. So, in order to most effectively make the parallel in this instance, it will be helpful to follow Freud's thinking on the matter, to demonstrate even more pertinent parallels and understanding of lyric composition. In working towards explaining the puzzle, Freud cites numerous examples, which indicate that dream-thoughts are essentially an interpretation of the dream-content, although, by definition, the dream-thoughts prompt the dream-content. The dream-content *represents* the dream-thoughts – indirectly, metaphorically, symbolically – as an "inherent psychical value", and in doing so, often uses elements that are not the same as in the dream-thoughts. Here again is evidence of a parallel with poetry, whereby the elements of the poem that represent the subterranean impulse for the poem, do so without explicitly expressing the central idea of the poem. To misuse Freud's words: "The *poem* is, as it were, differently centred from the unconscious – its content has different elements as its central point" (2004,

p. 410). What I am saying, more specifically, is that the underlying driver of Lysenko's poem is not the nostalgia of him and his brother playing in the house frame, nor is it the fact that his brother gets stuck in the chimney: it is his guilt at surviving his brother's heroin overdose death at a young age. Likewise, the underlying drive in McBryde's poem is his personal abandonment as a child, not the two sailors being lost or abandoned at sea.

In a further attempt to explain the phenomenon, Freud seems to touch on something that is essential and paradoxical in the process of composition, for dreams and for poetry:

> We shall be led to conclude that the multiple determination which decides what shall be included in a dream is not always a primary factor in dream-construction but is often the secondary product of a psychical force which is still unknown to us... It thus seems plausible to suppose that in the dream-work a psychical force is operating which on the one hand strips the elements which have a high psychical value of their intensity [*displacement*], and on the other hand, by *means of overdetermination*, creates from elements of low psychical value new values, which afterwards find their way into the dream-content. If that is so, *a transference and displacement of psychical intensities* occurs in the process of dream-formation, and it is as a result of these that the difference between the text of the dream-content and that of the dream-thoughts comes about. (2004, pp. 411–12)

This "transference and displacement of psychical intensities" could be argued to closely resemble the process of composition, whereby the poet, whether they are aware of it or not, transfers and displaces elements from their psyche, and, as a result distorts what they represent, through metaphor and metonymy. As to why they might do this, Freud again provides a possible clue:

> The consequence of the displacement is that the dream-content no longer resembles the core of the dream-thoughts and that the dream

> gives no more than a distortion of the dream-wish which exists in the unconscious... Dream-displacement is one of the chief methods by which that distortion is achieved ... We may assume, then, that dream-displacement comes about through the influence of the same censorship – that is, the censorship of endopsychic defence. (2004, p. 412)

It is here that I can diverge from Freud, on the back of this element of distortion through endopsychic censorship, and begin to directly contemplate the action of the lyric poet in composition. I propose this because logic suggests that the reasons for self-censorship in dreams may differ from those for self-censorship in poetry, even though both are being strongly, if not exclusively, influenced from the unconscious.

It seems possible to speculate that endopsychic censorship for the poet is the result of being wary of images that are too *connected*, images that overdo the suggestion; or they are seen as being too obvious or predictable or didactic; or where the poet even has the need to "fool" her or himself, or, more pertinently, to fool those who might read the poem and *know* exactly what it is they are actually saying. This may suggest that there is more conscious intent involved in this process, but it does not exclude the possibility that the unconscious is also engaged in endopsychic defence. My central point is that the unconscious is the predominant driver or reason for the poem, but it does not exclude the influence of consciousness. This is particularly the case when the third stage of composition, the review and reworking stage occurs. As I will show, in the cases of Lysenko and McBryde, the unconscious drive of the poems is paramount, and in both cases it is arguable that the endopsychic defence emanates from their unconscious need to avoid public scrutiny or else to protect or deny their own consciousness of the guilt, shame, despair, or anger that they feel. The avoidance of public scrutiny suggests that the unconscious may be capable of discerning, independent of consciousness, that some element needs to be hidden. Generally I would say that the poet is aware of this self-censorship, if not in the second, hyperconscious stage, at least in the third stage of review. However, as I will show, the cases of Lysenko and McBryde suggest greater powers of the unconscious influence over the conscious act of poetry, and perhaps generally. Generally speaking, however, even in the hyperconscious state, the poet has, if intermittently, the conscious critic, "controller" or censor *at their shoulder*, as if observing the unravelling elements of their psyche (dream/poem), keen to control the multifarious suggestions of the imagery in language, ensuring they are not overdone or clichéd, obvious or revealing, but at the same time focusing the poem on some central element, no matter how deliberately misleading, ambiguous or "challenging" this may be. The complete determinants of these elements are of course a mystery, even to the poet.

The "psychical forces" determining what is primarily emerging from the unconscious will undoubtedly be warped and blocked by the various and varying elements of consciousness at play in the hyperconscious flux. This is the psyche of the poet in the state of heightened focus: the "psychical force which is still unknown to us" (2004, p. 412). What needs to be added is language, or a means of expression. For this, the poet has prepared (and continues to prepare), with long reading and listening. In his letter to Demeny, Rimbaud suggests: "… if what he [the poet] brings back from *down there* has form, he gives form; if it is formless, he gives formlessness. A language must be found" (1966, p. 309). This "language" is the language of poetry. What this language is, is a question for another study, and which the scope of this dissertation cannot encompass.

Therefore, from the above part of this study, Freud's observations on the dream and the dreamer can be seen to indicate certain psychical processes paralleling the sleeping mind with the hyperconscious or unintention of the poet, such states indicating the *unknown* psychical forces driving the poem: the subterranean or unconscious drivers.

CHAPTER TWO

LACAN AND POETRY: JUMPING THE BAR

In Lacan's essay "The Instance of the Letter in the Unconscious or Reason since Freud" (2004), where he expands upon Freud's *The Interpretation of Dreams*, he examines the role of language in expressing the unconscious. At the outset he declares, "what the psychoanalytic experience discovers in the unconscious is the whole structure of language [and that] the notion that the unconscious is merely the seat of the instinct will have to be rethought" (2004, p. 447). By investigating this "rethink", I want to use Lacan to advance my idea of the predominance of the unconscious, and the language of the expression of that unconscious, that is not "merely the seat of the instinct", evidenced especially in lyric poetry, and that finds expression in the unintentional hyperconscious. As Lacan himself puts it: "I think of what I am where I do not think to think" (2004, p. 457). This is what I call the poet-paradox, which I will elaborate on in Chapter Five.

In his study, Lacan examines "the emergence of linguistic science" whereby:

> it is contained in the constitutive moment of an algorithm that is its foundation. This algorithm is the following:

$$\frac{S}{s}$$

> which is read as: the signifier over the signified, "over" corresponding to the bar separating the two stages. (2004, p. 448)

Lacan points out that the signifying chain has a "whole articulation of relevant contexts suspended 'vertically'" (2004, p. 451). This "chain" suggests that the nature of language is dependent upon the culture for its "chain" of meaning(s): the multitude of referents that words contain, that are inherent in the language. Lacan uses a segment from a Paul Valéry poem to illustrate the point, and he concludes with the following statement:

> But this whole signifier can only operate ... if it is present in the subject ... by supposing that it has passed over to the level of the signified.
>
> For what is important is not that the subject know anything whatsoever ...
>
> What this structure of the signifying chain discloses is the possibility I have ... to use it in order to signify *something quite other* than what it says. (2004, p. 452)

In other words, the language itself "knows" through the vertical chain, whether the subject is aware of it or not, and that it can say (signify) something else than what its apparent or surface meaning indicates. The name of this signifying function in language Lacan identifies as *metonymy*. "*One word for another*, that is the formula for the metaphor" (2004, p. 453, author's italics). To a poet or a reader of verse this seems obvious, but Lacan is examining the subjective power of language, and in doing so he is alluding not only to the "stuff" of poetry but to the parallel universe of Freud and the unconscious. Freud and Lacan's discovery is that the signifying chain is inherent in language, through the nature of metonymy/metaphor, and that this chain can break through the apparent bar between signifier and signified for the subject; for my purposes, this is as far as I need take this point.

The purpose of this dissertation should perhaps be reiterated here, taking the cue from Lacan and Freud: that the poet, being more than normally "aware" of the signifying chain of language, and its "whole articulation of relevant contexts suspended 'vertically'" (2004, p. 451), operates language consciously, but also unconsciously, in all possible variations and levels of absorption, producing literature whose complete interpretation not even the poet her or himself is completely capable of.

When Lacan points out that "[t]he linguistic structure that enables us to read dreams is the very principle of the 'significance of the dream'" (2004, p. 455), again, as with poetry, the dream/language is not what we read it to be, but what its inherent vertical chain suggests. Lacan summarises Freud's three elements of dream-thought, indicating how they "deal with the letter of the discourse, in its texture, its usage, its immanence" (2004, p. 455), so that the signifying chain of the letter is inherent in them (the dream-thoughts) in all its effects. In doing so he makes the same indication of these qualities within poetry, suggesting that poetry is discourse, in its broadest sense: the discourse of the unconscious, with the self and/or with the imagined listener.

Towards the end of "The Instance of the Letter in the Unconscious or Reason since Freud" (2004), Lacan points out that the "efficacy of the unconscious does not cease in the waking state. The psychoanalytical experience does nothing other than establish that the unconscious leaves none of our actions outside its field" (2004, p. 456). This statement suggests that the unconscious is active in all minds, and if this is so, then why is it that everyone is not a poet? The obvious answer to this is provided by this thesis: that it is the poet who is prepared (intentionally/vocationally) and practiced (in the hyperconscious) and skilled (in review). But these areas are learned actions, which suggests that there is something else that provokes the poet to be a poet, with the greater need and mechanism to express their thoughts and feelings, whether conscious or unconscious. I have no solid answer to this question, this "something else": the aim of this discourse is to establish the importance of the unconscious in the psychological state of the lyric poet, especially in the reaction to the creative impulse. I can guess that the lyric poet experiences a confluence of greater need and ability, both learned and natural, and opportunity to act and learn to act in the field of lyric verse, but I would also surmise that it is the need to speak in the way that is peculiar to the poet that is the greatest prerequisite.

Julia Kristeva has pointed to the existence of "signifying chains" that exist beyond language, beyond recognition, drives that initiate the first attempts at speech, that come from the first sense of loss, which she calls the semiotic *chora*:

> Discrete quantities of energy move through the body of the subject who is not yet constituted as such and, in the course of his development, they are arranged according to the various constraints imposed on this body – always already involved in the semiotic process –by family and social structures. In this way the drives, which are "energy" charges as well as "physical" marks, articulate what we call a *chora*: a nonexpressive totality formed by the drives and their stases in a motility that is as full of movement as it is regulated. (2002, p. 35)

These semiotic drives could be seen as analogical, parallel or at least somewhat connected to the unconscious drives that I am arguing instigate and complicate the poet's creative hyperconscious impulse to lyric-speak. This physical action of language may be the eventual expression that, in the poet, evolves in a particular and unique manner, the language of the poet. But it should be added here that, like the language of the poet, the *chora*, although identifiable in its general form, can never be understood as clear and evident. As Kristeva herself points out, "[a]lthough the *chora* can be designated and regulated, it can never be definitively posited: as a result, one can situate the *chora* and, if necessary, lend it a topology, but one can never give it axiomatic form" (2002, p. 35). And similarly, the unconscious, indeed the hyperconscious, drives can never be given axiomatic form. *That* they *are*, that they can be "designated and regulated" is undeniable; *what* they are, especially in any given instance, is not clear. We can identify and know the process or urge to create (to dream), and we can interpret this, but we cannot measure or formulate it.

CHAPTER THREE

THE EMBODIMENT OF EMOTIONS IN POETRY

If it can be accepted that the unconscious is a major, if not the major driver of the impulse to write lyric verse, it seems that the question then arises: what is it that the unconscious is attempting to express or to signify through poetic language (that the conscious cannot/does not)? David McCooey, in discussing what he terms "new lyricism", describes lyricism as: "what we associate most commonly with poetry: musicality; brevity; intensity; the drive to epiphany or insight; and an emphasis on thought, feeling and subjectivity" (2005, p. 69). It is this last notion of what is emphasised that I want to take up in the pursuing the understanding of what it is that the unconscious is expressing, and to investigate how this might or might not have changed over time.

It seems apparent that what the unconscious is expressing are the feelings and repressed memories of the subject, because it is these that are the most difficult to define or confront, let alone express. I think it could be said that thoughts are only difficult to conceptualise and articulate, whereas emotions are difficult because we cannot grasp exactly what they are and, more importantly, we are reluctant to reveal them to others. For this reason I would argue that it is the emotions that the unconscious is mostly expressing, in dreams and in lyric poetry, because it is the emotions, or what drives them that the consciousness has repressed, hidden, or otherwise avoided.

In his essay "Poetry and Consciousness", when discussing the difficulty of expressing emotions, the poet and scholar C. K. Williams not only alludes to the limitation of psychoanalytical language, but he expands on the need all humans have to reflect on and understand emotion:

> Mostly what we are doing when we are investigating an emotion is surrounding it, giving it a clearer background. That background can extend, in classical psychoanalysis, to the cradle, but as for the emotion we are experiencing itself, it can somehow not have been touched. (1998, p. 2)

In other words, when we examine emotions we are identifying the emotion in terms of its cause and effect, but we are not identifying or describing the emotion itself: what it is. Just as with "the unconscious", we can identify it as a concept, we can identify its effect, even guess at its causes, but we cannot say what it is. As Freud argued, we can only indicate it through what its symptoms are. Williams continues:

> The problem seems to arise when we have to describe ourselves to ourselves. For whatever reason, human consciousness is not satisfied with experience itself, it is our reflection on our experience that allows us to consider ourselves legitimated, that makes us recognise an emotion as authentic. (Williams, 1998, pp. 2–3)

This problem we have to describe "ourselves to ourselves" seems pertinent to the lyric poet, who has this need to express what they are feeling as themselves, and therefore and thereby to understand that feeling, that self. But more than the need, the lyric poet has the learned ability to express it, and perhaps they have a greater need to do so as well, so that they act upon the impulse and know how to react, how to express it: this is what makes a lyric poet. Rimbaud described a similar sentiment in his letter to Paul Demeny of 15 May 1871, when he declared, "The first study of the man who wants to be a poet is the knowledge of himself, complete. He looks for his soul, inspects it, tests it, learns it" (1966, p. 307). This looking for the knowledge of oneself seems akin to the need to describe ourselves to ourselves. But Rimbaud suggests that it is the first study of the poet, and perhaps this is because of the poet's greater need for this knowledge, combined with the poet's learned means and practice and other peculiar factors, such as inclination, adequate time, isolation, alienation, and/or idleness, so that it becomes a vocation, and is pronounced and prolonged.

For the lyric poet, reflection on a particular emotion – *what* it is – is not enough: it is *the experience itself* that the poet is driven to express. If the poet were to rely on investigating what the feeling is, they would not be discovering and describing "themselves to themselves" in the feeling, but merely naming it, providing a mere tag for the experiencer instead of "knowing" the experience. When it is felt deeply, the poet cannot express that experience except through the language that will evoke that feeling. And it is in this expressing of themselves through this feeling that the poet might be seen to be describing themselves to themselves. In other words the lyric poet needs to embody their emotions in their poetry, and in order to do so they must experience them in the writing of them, and thereby perhaps describe themselves to themselves.

Williams describes his mind as "a much more chaotic and turbulent phenomenon than those I've heard about: there is much more happening in it, much more happening at once, and much more happening in a nondetermined way" (1998, p. 3). This could well reflect the fluctuating psyche of most "normal" people's minds, and who is to say that the poet's mind is any more turbulent and chaotic? Perhaps the poet has the greater *need* to recover and redeem certain extreme feelings and ideas that occur in their psyche. This study is not concerned with the reasons why people turn to poetry, but I feel there is an important tangent here, that perhaps distinguishes the poet's psyche, in that they travel more often to the extremes of that psyche because they have, inherently, by practice, or both, the need (and the means) to do so.

Williams asserts that poetry embodies emotion "with great precision and rigor" (1998, p. 4). I am arguing here that the lyric poet's need to embody emotion springs from a vocational intention, an inherent and/or practiced preparedness, or *Negative Capability*, as Keats saw it (1952, p. 71). This is the intention to evoke feelings as they are experienced, from a position of receptivity, or hyperconsciousness, or unselfconscious passivity or submission; indeed with conscious absence, or egolessness.

In Keats' famous letter to his brothers on *Negative Capability* (1817), he could have been referring to the principle of intention and unintention, if we make allowances for the changing times and perspectives. Keats wrote:

> at once it struck me what quality went to form a Man of Achievement especially in Literature and which Shakespeare possessed so enormously–I mean *Negative Capability*, that is when man [*sic*] is capable of being in uncertainties, Mysteries, doubts, without any irritable reaching after fact and reason. (Keats, 1952, p. 71)

This "without any irritable reaching after fact and reason" seems to echo the unintention I am positing. For what else could it be that makes a person reach irritably for fact and reason but the ego or consciousness of the self? Or, conversely, what is it that might allow a person not to reach so, but to instead allow the psyche to be free of the conscious censor, in free association and drive, or at least relatively so (that is, without it being planned or formalised as in Automatic Writing), of the hyperconscious? In this state the psyche is "capable of being in uncertainties", indeed welcomes and utilises the mysteries and doubts in order to explore them without (or with as little as possible) prejudice (prejudgment). In an earlier letter to Benjamin Bailey, Keats wrote:

> I must say of one thing that has pressed upon me lately and encreased [*sic*] my Humility and capability of submission and that is this truth – Men of Genius are great as certain ethereal Chemicals operating on the Mass of neutral intellect – by (*for* but) they have not any individuality, any determined Character ... (1952, p. 66)

It is the phrase "capability of submission" that is key here, and for the purpose of this study it could be applied specifically to the habit or intention of submission (or availability) of the self to the unconscious impulse. Keats' idea of *Negative Capability* elaborated this notion of submission, and although he alludes to the general character of the "Man of Achievement" without specifically referring to the state of mind of the artist/poet in the act of creation, he could still be seen to be pointing to the same idea, especially when linked to the writings of Hazlitt. As David Bromwich points out:

> Keats found a clue for many of these speculations in the writings of Hazlitt ... The character of the artist is there said to be so absorbed in the act of creation that it subsists only inside the act. In the process of imagining, all the self-regarding data of ordinary life seem to vanish. (1993, p. 825)

Here, too, is the sense of the need for the artist to be free of the self-conscious, "self-regarding" self, the essential need to become absorbed, when the self has vanished in order for the hyperconscious to operate. And why does the poet create, but to, as Rimbaud put it, seek "the knowledge of himself, complete. He looks for his soul, inspects it, tests it, learns it ..." (307). This is the nub of the poet-paradox. Indeed, Rimbaud and Keats, and Hazlitt, seem to imply that this state must be habitually necessary and cultivated, until it is a *natural* state. Or, as Keats puts it, "they have not any individuality, any determined Character" (1952, p. 66), or Hazlitt: "The character of the artist … subsists only inside the act" (Bromwich, 1993, p. 825). Since Keats' time, now that there exists the "emphasis on the presentation of sensation and inner experience ... that turned nineteenth-century philosophy away from positivism and toward phenomenology (and) turned writers to the representation of experience *as* experienced by individuals" (Ferguson, 1996, p. 289), the character of the individual has gradually been seen as far more complex and multi-dimensional, where the subject, whether a fictional character or the non-artist or artist, can inhabit more than one personality, one character both in time and over time. This may explain the elementary point of difference between Keats' time and now. There is something of these notions of Keats and Hazlitt reflected in T.S. Eliot's determination of the need for a "continual extinction of personality" (p. 25), for which "the poet must develop or procure the consciousness of the past" (p. 25). Eliot is here referring to the history of poetry, "the main current, which does not at all flow invariably through the most distinguished reputations" (p. 24). For Eliot, in order for the poet to procure the consciousness of the past they cannot have a personality, nor invoke a personality, or else this will interfere with the procurement of the consciousness of the past. The poet is not expressing a personality but a medium "in which impressions and experiences combine in unexpected ways" (pp. 27–8). He writes, "It is a concentration which does not happen consciously or of deliberation" (p. 29). And so, how else must it occur, but unconsciously and unintentionally? I do not want to get into an evaluation or discussion of Eliot's ideas but present them as an echo of the principle of the poet's need for concentration, so that "[w]hat happens is a continual surrender of himself as he is at the moment to something which is more valuable" (Eliot, 1965, p. 25). Eliot completes section two of his essay with: "only those who have personality and emotions know what it means to want to escape from these things" (p. 29). Hence, in order to surrender and concentrate, the poet cannot afford to express her or his personality. What I am arguing is that the personality is a construct that may incorporate elements of what I call "the true self", but otherwise is too self-conscious to allow for the expression of the unconscious. In other words, the expression of the unconscious more and most readily represents an expression of the true self. By "the true self" I mean the self that exists without the intruding cognisance of self or personality, the self that can be said to exist from birth, before experience and knowledge develop and overwhelm the person and become them. This aligns somewhat with D.W. Winnicott's notion that the idea of the true and false self can be

> discerned in the early formulations of Freud. In particular [...] Freud's division of the self into a part that is central and powered by the instincts [...], and a part that is turned outwards and is related to the world. (p. 140)

I do not want to delve too deeply into this idea of the true and false self beyond it supporting my idea of the true self as an explanation for why the poet creates, and needs to do so, without the inhibition of her or his personality. To this end, Winnicott's notion is most useful, where he writes that "[a]t the earliest stage the True Self is the theoretical position from which come the spontaneous gesture and the personal idea [...] Only the True Self can be creative and only the True Self can feel real" (1965, p. 148). My idea of the personality being too self-conscious to allow the expression of the unconscious is somewhat akin to what Winnicott refers to as the False Self. Without going into his theory of its aetiology (and taken in its broadest terms), Winnicott's False Self hides the True Self so that the personality can function; in my view, and for the purposes of this discourse, the True Self enables the expression of the unconscious. As Winnicott puts it, conversely, "[t]he False Self, however well set up, lacks something, and that something is the essential central element of creative originality" (1965, p. 152). These ideas seem to fit in well with Eliot's idea that poetry is a "medium in which impressions and experiences combine in unexpected ways", and that the artist/poet may indeed have "personality" or "character" but they must learn to contain or "vanish" it in order to create, in composition.

THE CHANGING MANIFESTATION OF THE UNCONSCIOUS IN THE UNIVERSE OF QUANTA

Williams writes of the "nondetermined, apparently arbitrary phenomena generated by mind, both by way of image and language" as being the "foundation of the imagination" (1998, p. 5). In doing so, he admits that he seems to be conflicting with "the whole universe of psychology, particularly Freudian psychology". But he points out that "the universe in which Freud situated mind [*sic*] was a Newtonian universe, where phenomena could be accounted for with calculus and, by extension, in a cause-and-effect relationship". Whereas,

> [t]he universe in which we find our models is quite different. It is the universe of quanta, of events that bear a quality in themselves of a kind of indeterminateness ... in which the arbitrary, the unpredictable, undetermined event has a remarkable metaphoric similarity to that of quantum. (1998, p. 6)

This postmodern indeterminateness is reflected in what I am proposing as the increasing predominance of the unconscious in the creative impulse of lyric verse. In this universe of quanta consciousness has become increasingly uncertain and ungrounded. To put it another way, the compliant False Self has become increasingly uncertain and resulted in an increased and increasing need and facility for the True Self to express the unconscious drives. The recent history of poetry and poetics seems to have followed this curve away from certainty, in form and in content, into the free verse of modernism, into abstract lyricism, to the extremes of L-A-N-G-U-A-G-E Poetry and its offshoots and effects, in today's post-modern world.

The central point of Williams' essay is that it is poetry that is best suited to deal with this turbulence, what Terry Eagleton describes as the "contingent, ungrounded, diverse, instable, indeterminate" style of thought (vii), because poetry too is now more ungrounded, subterranean, driven by the indeterminate unconscious that is attempting to express emotions that are:

> in and of themselves, neither pure, spontaneous, nor very clear ... and if the soul is to do justice to their turbulence and furor without belittling itself, it must indeed be educated, and rigorously so. It is my thesis that the most useful method we have devised for that education is poetry. (Williams, 1998, p. 8)

In other words, the poet is best equipped, indeed educated, to educate the soul and the psyche to embody or realise the experience of emotion (and idea) in language and imagery. This education of the psyche is achieved through the praxis of reading and writing (and listening) that the poet undergoes. This is the "intention", the preparedness, the awaiting; the availability to the unintentional impulse or sudden need to speak (write) through the hyperconscious. Williams proposes that poetry is "as complicated, maybe more so, than an emotion" (1998, p. 8). He elaborates:

> It also shares many characteristics with emotion. It is composed of sensation, of image, language, a voice, perception, bodily reference, sentiment, morality, thought, and experience. It, like existence itself, concerns itself crucially with the arbitrary and the determined. (1998, p. 8)

In other words, poetry is in essence a chaotic and turbulent reflection of the psyche, expressed through the determinants of language and structure, and knowledge (education) of the latter is part of the necessary preparedness or intention to write.

CHAPTER FOUR

THE UNCONSCIOUS METAPHOR: THE HYPERCONSCIOUS IN ACTION

> We laymen have always been intensely curious to know ... from what sources that strange being, the creative writer, draws his material, and how he manages to make such an impression on us with it and to arouse in us emotions of which, perhaps, we had not even thought ourselves capable. Our interest is only heightened the more by the fact that, if we ask him, the writer himself gives us no explanation, or none that is satisfactory. (Freud 1908, p. 143)

The language used by Myron Lysenko in his poem "Chimney" (see below) is, at first sight, simple, even simplistic, and yet there emanates from the poem a feeling of considerable tension and feeling, conveyed by the imagery, the structure, and the short lines; and there is something more, some haunting quality that is not immediately identifiable but which drew me back to it, again and again. The poem's apparent appeal seemed to come from the simple, almost naïve language, the tension of the predicament of the poet's brother, and the short sharp lines, but there has always been for me an added intensity to it. Of course most lyric poems have this suggestion of deeper implication, but usually it can be gleaned with some close reading. In the case of Lysenko's poem, whenever I read it or heard Lysenko read the poem, the naivety of the language and the apparent simplicity of the narrative always disarmed my reading or hearing of it, and I never went further than the surface of the poem in understanding it. Eventually however, my close personal knowledge of Lysenko, and my knowledge of his brother's actual death led me to see the possibility of a deeper metaphorical resonance in the poem.

CHIMNEY

My brother
and I
were playing
hide and seek
around the
new houses
being built
down the road.
My brother
was hiding,
I couldn't
find him.
He called
and I
followed his
voice but
couldn't
see him.
I was
standing in
a house
without a floor.
I was sure
he was here,
somewhere.
I heard
shuffling sounds
come out
of the chimney.
move up
he couldn't
move down.
He was
stuck there
like an
Adam's Apple,
in the part
where the
chimney narrows.
I didn't
know what
to do
so I
ran home
and ate
a sandwich.
I told
my father
and we
ran back.
My father
pulled at
my brother's leg.
My brother
cried out.
The fire brigade
arrived but
couldn't help.
A crowd
was forming.
My brother
move down
until
bricklayers
came and
took the
top of
the chimney off
brick by
brick
taking care
not to
drop the
larger chunks
down the
chimney
while
my brother
waited there
suspended
in mid-chimney
coughing softly
and keeping
the dust
off his
eyes
with tears
as his
brown hair
bit by bit
turned grey
as little
by little

I looked up
the chimney
and he was
in there
stuck
halfway.
He couldn't

was there
stuck halfway
like an
Adam's Apple.
He couldn't
move up,
he couldn't

the sun
came in
to lighten
his day
and move
his body
away.

(Lysenko, 1998, p. 43)

My intention here is to analyse the poem, using the language of the poem in conjunction with the knowledge of the poet's personal life, as well as the personal observations of the poet some 15 years after he wrote it, to uncover a deeper unintended unconscious drive informing the poem, and to thus identify a concrete example of unconscious drive. I have made a similar enquiry into another poem by another Melbourne poet, Ian McBryde, which will be addressed later in the thesis.

Around 2001 when reading "Chimney" again, some six years after first encountering it (I had heard Lysenko read the poem quite a few times in the 90s and it was published in his collection *Winning and Losing* in 1998), I began to wonder about the connection of the poem to Lysenko's brother's death from a heroin overdose in 1991, especially as he had written it just a few years after, some time around 1993 or 1994. Lysenko had come to Sydney and had stayed with me when his brother was in a coma; he was still there when, after two or three days, his brother died. During this tragic and traumatic time, I remembered being a little surprised at the extent of Lysenko's grief at his brother's death. Grief is of course natural but there was, it seemed to me, something about Lysenko's reaction that was beyond what might have been expected. He was inconsolable. I can remember thinking this at the time, but it wasn't until reading the poem again and again, many years later that I began to think more of it, and see its possible deeper metaphorical inferences. Certain phrases began to take on greater significance: "I couldn't / find him",

"I / followed his / voice but / couldn't / see him", "I was / standing in / a house / without a floor", and (when he finally sees him) "he was / in there / stuck / halfway. / He couldn't / move up, / he couldn't / move down." The last series of lines is repeated in the poem. Anyone who has experienced the futility of trying to help or confront a friend or family member with an addiction, especially to heroin, might recognise the true significance of these lines. But as well as this, they might be read as reflecting Lysenko's feelings about his brother when he was in the coma. Later in the poem there is reference to Lysenko's brother being "suspended / in mid-chimney / coughing softly / and keeping the dust / off his / eyes / with tears / as his / brown hair / bit by bit / turned grey" and finally, "the sun / came in / to lighten / his day / and move / his body / away." Here, the choice of words is odd and significant: instead of writing, "move him away", Lysenko writes "move his body away": as one might write of a dead person. Once the connection is made, the inferences of death a slow and lonely death, in all these words and phrases seems obvious.

In 2001, in a casual conversation about writing, I asked Lysenko if, when he was writing the poem, the metaphor of his brother's heroin addiction and death was intentional; Lysenko was taken aback. He said this had not occurred to him, then or since, but now I had pointed it out he could see it. He was surprised he hadn't previously made the connection himself. He was understandably moved by this revelation.

Lysenko's brother is never named in the poem. Is it too painful to name him? Perhaps this is a mark of respect, an acknowledgment of his passing. The phrase "my brother" appears six times. The last lines of the poem are packed with significance: "the sun / came in / to lighten his day". His death (removal from the trapping and constricting chimney, which suggests heroin addiction and/or coma) lightens his day, because he no longer has the heavy duty of his addiction and all the sordidness that this involved.

A close friend, and someone whom Lysenko admired greatly, the poet Jas H. Duke, also died a year or so after Lysenko's brother, in June 1992. At Duke's funeral service and cremation Lysenko seemed fascinated with the cremation process, particularly with the chimney. I have asked Lysenko about the possibilities of the connection of this event with the poem "Chimney", and while he says he remembers his fascination with the cremation chimney, he isn't sure about the connection. If there is a connection, it is not a conscious one.

A particular, perhaps telling slip occurs in "Chimney" in the first column, where at one point Lysenko suddenly slips from the past to the present tense: "I was sure / he was here / somewhere". Indeed this whole passage is full of possible allusions, highlighted by the enjambment: "I was sure": Implying that Lysenko was once sure, but he is now no longer so. The lines "standing in / a house / without a floor" suggests the uncertainty of even the floor of a house (representing the family / siblings / security / life). Perhaps it is a reflection of the terrible feeling Lysenko had when his brother was in the coma in Sydney: when he was not sure that his brother would live. But after his death, when he is writing the poem, Lysenko's memory of his brother and the connected guilt and regret is present, in the present tense. Either the guilt attached to his brother is still present, (and/) or else Lysenko's memory of the episode is so sharp still, that it is as if it is in the present: "I was sure / he was here / somewhere". The "was" and "here" reflect this conflicted memory of the sureness of his brother being present, at least "somewhere".

The accentuated enjambment and shortening of the lines slows the narrative, making the reader stop and move their eyes to the next line, interrupting the flow and envisaging of the poem, and at the same time reflecting the frustration and helplessness and tension for Lysenko. Ostensibly it seems Lysenko has done this because the lines, in creating three columns, look like chimneys. Indeed, he has informed me that this was his reasoning. However I would suggest that instinctively (unconsciously) he has used the short, enjambed lines also for the reasons suggested, to slow the pace of the narrative, and because they reflect his deep sense of helplessness, uncertainty and guilt, even when he is not aware that this is the case.

In a subsequent discussion with Lysenko in 2002, some time after my initial discussions of the poem's deeper implications in 2001, he informed me that his mother had since accused him of "lying" in the poem, saying that his brother was not hiding in a game of hide-and-seek, but that he (Lysenko) had actually dared his brother to go up the chimney. I asked Lysenko if this was true and he shook his head uncertainly, saying that he might have, but he couldn't remember. "It's the sort of thing I did," he said. "Daring him to do things like that. He was incredible, fearless. He amazed me the things he'd do. I never really thought he would do them when I dared him, but he nearly always did". This kind of influence and dominance, even hero-worship, is common for a younger brother, but it can hardly be seen as a cause for culpability. What is arguable is that the unconscious might hold onto and develop these connections and, subsequently, create a prolonged sense of guilt.

Upon examining the poem again, I recalled that whenever Lysenko read it at a live reading it always got a lot of laughs, and I began to wonder why. Apart from the fact that someone stuck in a chimney might be somewhat amusing, it wasn't that funny, and now that I had touched on a possible tragic subtext it was even more puzzling. I noticed that the first half of the poem was quirky but not comic. Then I came to the seven-line phrase in the middle of the poem, especially the four lines that end it: "I didn't / know what / to do / so I / ran home / and ate / a sandwich" which seems to alter the whole tone of the poem (it certainly does so whenever Lysenko reads the poem). When I asked Lysenko about the inclusion of this phrase, some time in 2002, he nodded and said:

> Yes. It wasn't in the poem at first. I was reading it one night and half way through it felt too slow and sad, so I just put that phrase in, and everyone roared with laughter, and the poem changed!

It might be arguable that this humorous insert was a conscious attempt to relieve Lysenko's own deeper, unconscious feelings of grief and guilt about his brother's death, his conscious or ego overriding his unconscious or indeed, his superego, as if to say: I don't want this sadness and guilt, leave me alone. When he made the insertion is even more pertinent – during the tense, highly charged atmosphere of reading to a live audience – yet absorbed in reading the poem, re-living the poem, even though he is aware of the audience and their reaction (or lack of it), Lysenko experiences those subterranean feelings and his conscious self wants to override them. This surely is a clear example of Freud's "relief theory" when the superego allows the ego to generate humour, or when the saving of some psychic energy is then discharged through laughter. Freud explains it thus: "in a particular situation the subject suddenly hypercathects his super-ego and then, proceeding from it, alters the reactions of the ego" (1985, p. 432). According to Freud, this process can be equally applied to humour whereby "humour would be the contribution made to the comic through the agency of the superego" (1985, p. 432).

A short time after establishing these subterranean drives in Lysenko's poem, I was reading Ian McBryde's book *Equatorial* when I came to the poem "Last Fathom", a narrative imagining of two sailors who while working on the conning tower in 1987, their submarine dived without them, ten nautical miles south-east of Sydney. The divers' plight was only realised some time later and their bodies were never recovered. As with Lysenko's poem, I was alerted to the close metaphorical connection to McBryde, whom I also knew personally. McBryde is an orphan who has written numerous poems directly about his feelings about and for his biological father who abandoned him and his mother when he was a baby, and which led to him being brought up in an orphanage. McBryde is still openly, fiercely hostile and resentful of his biological father about this. In a conversation some time in 2004, when I asked him if the metaphor of the sailors was deliberate, he said he didn't know what I meant. When I asked him what the poem was really about, he said it was about two sailors who had been left behind, etc. but when I pointed out that the poem was surely about "abandonment" he was momentarily speechless, and confessed he had not realised the connection, but now I had pointed it out he could see that this had undoubtedly been what had *made* him write about the sailors. There is not the same signifying language in McBryde's poem that there is in Lysenko's, but the underlying driver and the symbolism is there: the authority of the submarine (the father – I cannot entirely resist the phallic suggestion of the submarine) abandoning the sailors in the sea (mother?) where they are lost and slowly drown. As with "Chimney", the short, sharp lines and simple language carry the reader into and along with the poem. But in a different way from the Lysenko poem, here there is the shockingly tragic story disarming any need to investigate any deeper personal message.

I am not sure if McBryde had a younger brother, but he is likely to have become friends with other orphaned boys who would have felt similarly abandoned. The poem is narrated by the elder sailor, Crow, and one line, towards the end, "I forgive everyone" (p. 26), seems oddly out of context. But when the underlying metaphoric notion is accepted this phrase is no longer odd. Other references are also pertinent, but seem perfectly suitable in the surface context of the story: "*Crow tell her. / Tell my mother.*"* (2001, p. 24), and the final two lines: "I can stay afloat/until someone comes" (2001, p. 27).

Both of these poems have lyrical elements, in that both are intense, both offer some metaphoric complexity, and both employ a personal voice.

* Speech in the poem is written in italics.

However, in both poems this personal voice is not the close personal voice of the poet: Lysenko's poem is his anecdote, his voice, but the voice is not deeply personal, whereas McBryde's voice is deeply personal but it is an assumed voice, that of Crow, one of the missing sailors. And yet, as I have shown, when we investigate the metaphorical underpinnings of the poems, their deep lyrical drive and substance becomes evident, as does the deep personal connection to the poets: each poem is expressing through unintentional metaphor their author's deeply troubling past. The major difference is that Lysenko has chosen the subject of his brother, and their formative relationship, which is in fact what the poem is about, but on a deeper, more complex level, whereas McBryde's subject is someone he does not even know, but for whom he apparently feels a profound affinity, an affinity that is prompted by the connection with his own early childhood, a prompting that he is not aware of until the connection is suggested to him, well after the poem has been published. Strikingly, both poems use similar language and line structure: simple words, short syllables, short, dramatic, enjambed lines that slow and intensify the inherent psychological pain. And both poets were of a similar age, in their forties, when they wrote the poems: an age that might be seen as a time of reflection.

I am not sure how far I can say that this evidence of the unconscious at work exists in all or indeed any of these two poets' other works, let alone to what extent it exists in other lyric poets' work. What I am saying is that it suggests the possibility of the importance, if not the essentialness, of the unconscious, manifested through the hyperconscious, in the operation of the lyric impulse.

In 1933, in his essay "Psychology and Literature", Carl Jung suggested that consciousness was like a helpless observer swept along by its unconscious, just as McBryde and Lysenko seem to have been:

> Whenever the creative force predominates, human life is ruled and moulded by the unconscious as against the active will, and the conscious ego is swept along on a subterranean current, being nothing more than a helpless observer of events. (1952, p. 197)

Just a few years after his brother's death, Lysenko's conscious ego recalled and imagined that day of exploration with his brother, a day that represents their childhood, and his writing it down was driven by the creative force of the unconscious, sweeping him along on its subterranean current of grief and regret and guilt.

In his essay, "On Lyric Poetry and Society", Theodor W. Adorno, when prefacing his examination of the lyric poem and society, identifies the essence of the lyric as

> [when] immersion in what has taken individual form elevates the lyric poem to the status of something universal by making manifest something not distorted, not grasped, not subsumed. It thereby anticipates, spiritually, a situation in which no false universality, that is, nothing profoundly particular, continues to fetter what is other than itself, the human. The lyric work hopes to attain universality through unrestrained individuation. (1991–92, p. 38)

This "unrestrained individuation" that affords a universality without it being "distorted … grasped [or] … subsumed" suggests a degree of focus that is unaware of its larger implications. By this focus on the subject matter being examined in the poem, the self is free to be, and hence achieve a universality that would otherwise be contrived and "fettered". This is a notion that will be examined further, in chapter five, by examining the paradoxical state of the lyric poet in transcending his or her self in order to express him or herself: what I call the poet-paradox.

Although I am chiefly concerned with the impetus or origin of the impulse to write the lyric, and not an analysis of the genre, these words of

Adorno's point towards the need for the examination of the individual and the individual poem for their universality without the need to *distort* or *subsume* it. Lysenko's and McBryde's universality has been outlined in the above examination of the two poems. It has been demonstrated that in these poems they have achieved the unrestrained-ness necessary to attain the lyric because they have been operating so much through their unconscious drives. Can we call this an unconscious spontaneity? Perhaps as their demonstrably subterranean urges have been identified it can be argued that this true or truer reason for the poems' existence was spontaneous, as its true or at least essential substance was without conscious intent.

THE NEW LYRIC: JUNG'S PSYCHOLOGICAL AND VISIONARY CREATION IN THE POSTMODERN WORLD

In the chapter "Psychology and Literature" in his 1933 book *Modern Man in Search of a Soul* (Jung, 1952), Carl Jung's views on the creative process as either psychological or visionary may be useful for indicating the changes that have taken place in general in western lyric poetry since the time of the Romantics.* For Jung, the psychological mode reflects consciousness laid bare, a kind of Romantic and/or lyrical, realistic, unselfconscious outpouring:

> The psychological mode deals with materials drawn from the realism of human consciousness – for instance, with the lessons of life, with emotional shocks, the experience of passion and the crises of human destiny in general – all of which go to make up the conscious life of man, and his feeling life in particular ... The poet's work is an interpretation and illumination of the contents of consciousness ... they fully explain themselves. (1952, p. 211)

* For his discussion Jung was examining Goethe's Faust, which of course is not a lyric poem, but for my purposes the principle of the creative process is still useful.

Jung's view of the alternate mode, the visionary, is of material that is more opaque and complex, indeed more obliquely personal, where "the prodigious richness of the imaginative material has so overtaxed the poet's formative powers that nothing is self-explanatory and every verse adds to the reader's need of an interpretation" (1952, p. 210).

I suggest that the contemporary lyric poet has become a personification of this visionary mode, albeit often in a subtle, misleading manner. The work has thus become increasingly self-conscious or "more obliquely personal", so that "nothing is self-explanatory" (1952, p. 210), unless and if the poet writes a somewhat disguised lyric such as Lysenko or McBryde have done, without being consciously aware of it. Lysenko and McBryde have unconsciously avoided the need to be obliquely personal, but their poems are no less personal. But Lysenko and McBryde may be exceptional in the manner of their "avoidance". For many contemporary poets, there seems to be a prevalent self-consciousness driving an avoidance of deeply personal subject matter in their poems. David McCooey describes his notion of a new lyricism in Australian poetry as "both faithful and unfaithful to poetry. It is musical and so forth, but generally in a more self conscious way" (2005, p. 69). McCooey also describes his idea of a new lyricism in Australian poetry as "a form of lyricism that is simultaneously a reinvigoration of the lyric mode and a critique of it" (2005, p. 66). I would suggest that perhaps this critique is a reflection of the self-consciousness, the wariness, indeed the mistrust of the form while at the same time writing it. In an interview in 1993, Australian poet John Forbes made a kind of allusion to this wariness, or "chariness", even though he was referring specifically to Romanticism. The same attitude could be said to apply to the writing of the too obviously personal poem:

> Well I don't think I ever felt *le sang de la poèt* – in the full sense of "the blood of the poet courses in the veins". Because I've always been very chary of Romantic identifications. I don't have enough sense of

> self-confidence to be a Romantic – um, but I understand why people are – and I feel happy for them (tiny-brained fools). (1993, p. 95)

The visionary material of the poet that Jung describes is "no longer familiar. It is a strange something that derives its existence from the hinterland of man's mind" (1952, p. 211). Contemporary poets rarely make the substance of today's lyric obvious. I have already gone into detail about poets such as Lysenko and McBryde being so consciously wary, that their unconscious drives the material for them, and they, innocently, see it as anything but an outpouring of their unconscious, when in fact it is more revealing than they might ever have guessed. Could it be that these are the only two examples of such an unconscious drive? I doubt it, but I cannot speculate or investigate other poets and their poems because to do so would require the same privileged personal knowledge and access. I am not suggesting the need for such an investigation in order to interpret or understand contemporary poems. What I am concerned with is the understanding of the psychology and process of the lyric impulse. As Jung himself says:

> The obscurity as to the sources of the material in visionary creation is very strange ... We are even led to suspect that this obscurity is not unintentional. We are naturally inclined to suppose – and Freudian psychology encourages us to do so – that some highly personal experience underlies this grotesque darkness. (1952, p. 213)

In Lysenko's poem "Chimney", even the obscurity itself is obscured, and the grotesquery is veiled: we are presented with something ostensibly mundane and autobiographical, reflecting childhood innocence, but beneath the little anecdote of the boy stuck in the chimney is a large grotesquery. This is perhaps an extreme development of what Jung is alluding to, where the intentionality of the obscurity is an unconscious intentionality. I don't want to suggest that this is the norm for the new lyric, but that, as an extreme, it suggests its possibility, and the direction this trend can take.

Many other contemporary lyric poets are simply doing what Jung describes, if self-consciously, snidely, where their cynicism hides their embarrassment or fear of being sentimental or earnest or obvious, or "hysterical", as Forbes puts it, albeit ironically (self-consciously), in his poem "Anti-Romantic":

You meet your daemon &
respond with contempt

for all depth & poetry
driven by love and breath

self-conscious bitterness
is best, besides lust or a

detached disgust–as
long as there's nothing

hysterical about it Art
& life both require this

but your attitude like
inspiration disappears,

leaves you ugly & stranded,
the moment you admire it.
(1998, p. 162)

Whatever the intention of the poet, what they are producing is "uncanny", because like most poets, they do not want to be familiar. In his 1919 essay "The 'Uncanny'", Freud made an extensive effort to define the term using dictionaries and various languages, as well as a number of case studies where the term had been used. The result is far from certain in defining the term. The best that can taken from Freud's study is in his discussion of the

German word *unheimlich* that has been translated into English as "uncanny": this word in German translates as unhomely, or "the opposite of what is familiar" (Freud, 2001, p. 931). Freud goes on to reason that because not all things that are unfamiliar are frightening, "We can only say that what is novel can easily become frightening and uncanny" (1919, p. 931). Through his discussion of Nicholas Royle's book *The Uncanny*, McCooey clarifies the term when he writes: "The uncanny has to do with strangeness, eeriness. But to define it is paradoxical, since it is also about a troubling of definitions. We can find in it the unfamiliarity of the familiar, or in the sense of the familiar in the unfamiliar" (McCooey, 2005, p. 67). Many contemporary lyric poets are writing the uncanny in this paradoxical range of the unfamiliar because they want to unsettle the given, they want to challenge the familiar, they want what is seen, to be seen anew: they want to de-familiarise the known. To extend this notion, I suggest that the contemporary poet does not want to be obvious or transparent with it. They have learned through the experience of their predecessors and history that the work does not really change anything; society continues on its flawed way, no one is listening, truly listening (or at least not enough are) so what is the point of being "obvious"?

In McCooey's analysis of the key concerns of Australian contemporary poetry, he cites the uncanny as another trope (New Lyricism being one), and in doing so he quotes Royle to explain that "[i]t [the uncanny] can consist in a sense of homeliness uprooted, the revelation of something unhomely at the heart of hearth and home" (Royle quoted by McCooey, 2005, p. 67). Is it not remarkable that not only is there a proven sense here of the concealed drivers in Lysenko's poem, but the subject matter is literally about "something unhomely at the heart of hearth and home"? The definition of *hearth* being "the floor of a fireplace" (McCooey, 2005, p. 67). It is as if Lysenko has read Royle's book and McCooey's article and fashioned his poem "Chimney" accordingly, except that both book and article were written ten and twenty years respectively after Lysenko's poem.

From all of this it might seem an obvious development, as poets perceive and familiarise themselves with their predecessors, that they should feel a need, intentional or not, to become more obscure, to find ways of covering their tracks, ways of challenging their readers, to avoid, at all costs, the crime of triteness, or worse, sentiment or obviousness. This is not a new thing, as has been noted by, among others, the Formalist Victor Shklovsky, who called it defamiliarisation.

Jung suggests that the artist resorts to mythological themes to express deeper feelings, and although it is true that poets still use mythological themes and images they are becoming less and less common, something that is resisted as overused or irrelevant, as Greek, Roman, Egyptian and Biblical referents become less known and/or less relevant or popular, especially in our multicultural, eclectic post-modern world. This may explain this newer mix where the hero is dead: long live the individual as his own flawed hero, or anti-hero. "The psychological disposition of the poet himself [may] take us away from the psychological study of the work of art" (Jung, 1952, p. 214), but in this dissertation I want to emphasise how the psychology of the work of art expresses the psychological disposition of the poet at the time of impulse, even if they (the poet) envisages or thinks otherwise at the time of writing. Indeed, the outcome and implications for the poet can become the opposite of what they envisage at the time of the writing of the poem. I am avoiding the term "intend" here, in its conventional sense, as I don't want to confuse it with my notion of intention in the process of lyric composition. Rimbaud was a fine poet in his late teens (his first poem was published when he was just sixteen), and arguably became naturally prepared to be so after schooling from an early age in Latin verse from his strict Catholic mother,* as well as

* Rimbaud's mother "punished her sons by making them learn a hundred lines of Latin verse by heart and if they gave an inaccurate recitation, she would deprive them of meals"

through private tutors. My argument is that this was the fundamental period of intention for Rimbaud, when he became prepared to write. This notion of intention is a key part of my argument, so I will quote Shklovsky here, even though he is using the word "intention" in its more generally accepted sense: "Art processes the ethics and world view of a writer and liberates itself from his original intention" (1977, p. xiii, quoted by Richard Sheldon in the Introduction to "Third Factory"). The implication here is that the poem is so driven by forces other than the conscious intention of the poet that it takes on a complex mix of their ideas and feelings, conscious and unconscious, and is often eventually not what was intended. Hence my notion of the unconscious and all it contains driving the poem at the time of impulse: the second stage in the compositional process of the lyric.

The examination of the psychology of the poet has led us inevitably to the study of psychology, of Jung and of course to Freud before him. In the examination of the work, or of the artist through the work, the psychoanalyst adopts a similar approach to the critic, or scientific analyst. Rather than the examination of the process of creation itself, in general and particular, it is the psychological mechanisms that Freud identifies. But it is these mechanisms that are useful in identifying the evidence of the make-up of the unconscious. But what is it that sets the mechanisms off? What is it that triggers the unconscious need to "speak"?

EPIPHANIC MOMENTS

In most cases, it could be said, and has been said, that it is the epiphanic moments which create those states of illumination that compel the poet to write, where most people, even if they have these moments, are not so compelled. But why is this? Why is it that only the poet is driven to write?

(Rickword, 1971, p. 4).

The short answer is that the lyric poet is *intending* to write, has prepared to do so, even if they are not consciously doing so. Robert Langbaum provides a more elaborate and articulate distinction:

> It is the sensitized condition of the observer that brings on epiphany, and the art of epiphany consists in establishing this sensitized condition. For epiphany offers insight into the observer as well as into the object observed. (1978, p. 37)

I interpret this as suggesting that the predilection for writing poetry is created and intensified by the preparation of sensibility (what I call intention) to the impulse to write (unintention). This leads to the final chapter, where I want to examine the poet, or observer, in the state of the hyperconscious, and the paradox this creates.

CHAPTER FIVE

THE POET-PARADOX: UNINTENTION AND THE EMBODIMENT OF *EMOTIONAL TRUTH*

In the previous chapters I have aimed to establish the notion of the hyperconscious in the writing of lyric poetry, by explaining what I call intention and unintention in the process of lyric composition. I have done this by establishing the importance of the unconscious, in Freudian terms, sourced through the unintention of the poetic state of hyperconsciousness in the writing of the lyric poem. I have also described the term intention as the educational and vocational preparedness to be available to the impulse to write. Lysenko and McBryde's poems are extreme examples of the evidence of this, as they seem to be driven not by the apparent, obvious content of the poems but by deep-rooted, subterranean personal forces. Beyond identifying the existence of the hyperconscious, with some explanation as to what it incorporates, I cannot be axiomatic about its make-up. This leads us back to the poets themselves, and to poetry commentators, to see if we can determine clearly, or at least expansively, the existence of this psychic state and its implications for the writing of lyric poetry. Key to this determination is what

I call the *poet-paradox*: the notion that the self can be most vividly and truly represented only when the poet is not "present", in the peculiar focus of the poetic state; when the poet is least self-conscious.

I will at the outset of this chapter speculate on just what it is that lyric poetry is expressing, in general terms, and why it is that the difficulty or peculiarity of this expression generally necessitates a focal state of unintention in hyperconsciousness and through this, the engagement of the unconscious. It is arguable that it is the emotional state that the lyric poet is mostly attempting to signify. However it is my contention that thoughts or ideas are in a sense an emotion of the mind or psyche, and can be included in this notion of "emotions". *Emotion* is usually regarded as strong feeling or instinctive or intuitive feeling, and *feel* comes from Old Norse *fălma* to grope, Latin *palma* palm (Collins, 1981): and so it follows that a thought could be regarded as a feeling or "groping" or emotion of the (palm/hand of) the mind.

It seems a natural progression to ask from this, why do people have this feeling (in terms of both emotion and thought), or "groping", and why do poets have the compulsion to express it the way they do? My position is that the poet is at their most potent when they are most unselfconscious: when they are unintentionally writing, when the feeling, the idea, the impulse takes hold of them, when the poet is "not present", when they are "someone else", when they may not even know exactly what it is that they are expressing, because it is then that the deeper and stronger felt emotions and ideas emerge, which is why they are subterranean/hidden/denied. The examples of Lysenko and McBryde are extreme cases used here to establish this unconscious-via-un-self-consciousness: if these poets were to attempt to write poems about those central issues (Lysenko's brother's death by drug overdose, and McBryde's feelings of abandonment upon reading about the sailors) the poems would be less powerful, less convincing, because of the risk that the poets would be too "present", too aware of themselves, too self-conscious, and therefore not truly themselves: they would be writing *as* themselves not *through* themselves.

This notion that the poet does not, indeed need not, understand what they are truly writing about is well expressed by Rimbaud in the letter to Paul Demeny of 15 May 1871, when he wrote that: "a song is so seldom a work, that is to say, a thought sung and understood by the singer. For *I* is someone else. If the brass wakes up a trumpet, it is not its fault" (1966, p. 305). The poet "wakes up" or becomes their true(r) selves when they are in the poetic state of composition. Lysenko and McBryde are brass woken up as trumpets because they were not self-conscious, because they unwittingly plumbed their unconscious depths, because they had "prepared", by their intention, because of their need to write their deeply personal poetry.

Jean Cocteau, writing in *Opium – The Diary of a Cure*, declared that "Once a poet wakes up, he is stupid, I mean intelligent. 'Where am I?' he asks. Notes written by a poet who is awake are not worth much" (1980, p. 90). Here too, Cocteau is acutely aware of the requirement of the poet to be "stupid", but what does he mean by this? He is relating stupidity to intelligence, in the sense that to be truly intelligent one must have no prejudice (pre-judgement), especially of oneself, and in order to achieve this, one must relinquish all prior knowledge. This accords with this dissertation's position that "innocence" or "un-self-consciousness" is required of the poet. Cocteau is of course being ironic, but serious too, in suggesting that it is only when the poet is stupid (innocent and ignorant) that they are "awake" enough to speak truly, without prejudice, particularly without prejudice of themselves: when I is someone else.

With the nature of the psychology of the poet in composition identified at least in general terms, with the inherent limitations of such identification acknowledged, I will now extend this study to attempt to understand more clearly, more particularly what is occurring during the creative state. I will do this by examining evidence of individual poets' praxis, out of which I might make a more substantial claim for principle.

HYPERCONSCIOUS PRAXIS

The varying degree or intensity to which the state of hyperconsciousness exists between poets (as well as between poems) means it cannot be defined or determined in exact terms. It will depend upon, among other things, the subject matter of the poem, and the personality, mood, circumstances of the poet and their environment at the time of composition. What is argued here is that this state of psychic focus exists to some degree, usually a great degree, and the poet is more likely to express their deeper, keener feelings and thoughts because the poet is least self-conscious in the act, and is, to some extent, *absent*. The argument here is that conscious or self-conscious feelings and thoughts are normally under the scrutiny of the self, and are thus less likely to be uninhibited, freely or truly expressed. The assumption is that no matter how bold, or how much the poet is convinced that no-one will read these thoughts and feelings, arguably, they are always conscious of the possibility on some level, unless the focal intensity of the hyperconscious is engaged. As has been suggested already, the term unconscious cannot be clearly defined, but as a concept it can be acknowledged, for it is used by psychoanalysts, academics, critics and artists, even those who are part of C.K. Williams' contemporary "universe of quanta" (1998, p. 6), in discussing the process and psychology of composition. Therefore, it may be useful, generally, in identifying a major driver of the hyperconscious. It should be acknowledged, of course, that it follows from this that the hyperconscious too, cannot be defined. It is the contention of this dissertation that it can, however, be identified as existing. And if the hyperconscious can be identified as existing it might be possible to recognise the nature and effect of it in the making of a poem. It might also be possible to identify how this effect varies between poets (and indeed between poems by the same poet).

A major question arising from these observations is this: why is the engagement of the hyperconscious necessary for the action of the creative impulse? What peculiar psychic quality does it evoke in the poet that enables the profound and illuminating work of the lyric poem?

Before I investigate this question, I want to iterate that it is assumed that intention in the compositional process qualifies the poet as a bona fide lyric poet. I do not want to argue for or against the merit of this or that bona fide lyric poet or movement of poets. My purpose is to investigate the process and thereby explore the possible psychology of composition, not the merit or efficacy of certain poets or poetry.

The American scholar Bo Earle makes some pertinent observations on this question of the need for the poet's *absence* or not self-conscious in order to express their deeper, keener feelings and thoughts. He does so mainly through an examination of the poetry and thoughts of Baudelaire, and the poet's need to lose himself in order to be himself in his art: what I call the poet-paradox. Earle opens this section of his 2006 study with a quote from Hegel:

> ... *tarrying with the negative is the magical power that converts* [the negative] *into being.* (Earle, 2006, p. 19, author's italics)

This quote alone, especially in the context of lyric poetry, suggests a negative or passive (in Keats' terms, "submissive"), receptive psyche for the poetic state or hyperconscious. This is the state of unintention when the poet is perhaps (most) alone, quiet, meditative, withdrawn, introspective, distracted; or else where they have developed such a receptive state even when among others, in traffic, climbing a mountain. It is in this state that the conscious self is more easily negated or diminished. In Williams' terms, this kind of negative "tarrying" enables the poet to embody the emotions in the poem because they are "absent" – because they are withdrawn from themselves. It is then the "magical power" occurs.

Earle writes:

> Yet it is precisely in virtue of experiencing, on one level, this perpetual, infinitely "multiplying" loss effected by the attempt to remember that the consciousness, or the "cœur tendre" (tender heart),* may, on another level, "grasp itself" precisely in the "ecstatic proliferation" of that loss itself. The poet does not only lose himself in perpetually self-negating attempts to remember, these attempts also have the effect "d'établir au-dessus de l'abîme une transcendence" (float above the abyss). This effect is born of the fact that the poet is not only consumed in his multiplying self-negation but also recognizes himself in the "ecstatic proliferation of that multiplication itself". (2003, p. 1021)

While in the focused state of composition, the poet loses themselves; however, paradoxically, in the process of transcendence, they find themselves. Compare this with Rimbaud's "For *I* is someone else" (1966, p. 305). As already suggested, this process is not fixed; the poet's psyche is quickly alternating various stages of consciousness, self-consciousness and un-self-consciousness in the *moment* of composition. The psyche is not a fixed, definable state (for poets or non-poets). But there is enough "escape" for them to lose and thereby *know* (write) themselves, in their psyche and through their language. This may be the difference between the poet and the non-poet: the latter may experience these moments of non-being, of "*I* is someone else", but they do not dwell upon them or have the need (or

* These loose translations in brackets after the French are mine. There are no translations of the French in Earle's original text. The term "cœur tendre" comes from Baudelaire's poem "Evening Song".

learned ability) to express them in poetry.

> Thus the poet's consciousness does not only lose itself with the setting sun but also finds itself anew in the "distance" that, with the sun's setting, engulfs all possible objects of consciousness: the poet "se prolonge" (is extended) precisely into this distance. He does not merely lose himself or fall into this distance, but also finds himself in the very movement, the coherence internal to such loss or falling itself, which Baudelaire here likens to a "valse mélancolique et langoureux vertige" (gloomy dance and languorous head-spin). This is a dance performed by the "sons" (sounds) and "parfums" of "vibrating" flowers that intermingle and "tournent dans l'aire du soir",[†] (turn in the night air) but also by the "cœur tendre" of the poet himself which is "afflicted" by an analogous "trembling". (Earle, 2006, pp. 1021–2)

In other words, it is in this "dance" that the poet finds herself or himself composing: the poem is a profound, *unintentional* reflection of the poet. The 'gloomy dance and languorous head-spin' suggests well the trance-like state of the composing mind, the spin perhaps of alternating *minds* that make up the individual and individuated psyche of the poet at the time of the inspired moment, this loss of self that accompanies the dream- or trance-like psyche in composition. And in this "dance", this "languorous head-spin" of the evening air, the self "evaporates": "In virtue of emitting such vibration and perfume the flower is said to 's'évaporer' (evaporate) in the evening air" (Earle, 2006, p. 1022). But at the same time the self is retrieved or realised in the act of transcendence that is composition:

> but this self-dispersal is simultaneously a self-retrieval due to the rhythmic coherence of the movement of dispersing itself. In turn, the poet is no longer a passive spectator of self-loss but an active participant in the "languid" and "melancholy", yet nonetheless rhythmically coherent and controlled "waltz" of self-losing. What the poet has

† Earle cites Baudelaire's poem as *"l'aire"* (the area) whereas in most poems it is *"l'air"* (the air), which also makes more sense.

> transcended, finally, is the simple dichotomy of self-presence and self-absence, for he finds himself now in the spiraling motion itself in which the one perpetually folds back upon the other. (Earle, 2006, p. 1022)

This spiralled, folding back transcendence of self-presence and self-absence is both a presence and an absence: the poet is present physically, and yet they are absent because their focus and engagement with their unconscious (whether they know it or not) means that they are not present. This is the poet-paradox.

The poet in the state of poetic creation is experiencing the unselfconscious discovery of her/himself: the sound and perfume of his or her essence disperses in the evening air, but that it exists means it is *known* (felt, experienced). Again, note Kafka's letter to Felice: "Writing means revealing oneself to excess" (Kafka, 1992, pp. 183–4). And further on in the same letter: "This is why one can never be alone enough when one writes. Why there can never be enough silence around when one writes, why even the night is not enough". The Australian author and journalist Martin Flanagan has articulated this paradox in a prosaic but clear manner thus:

> The creative path is dark, groping, essentially mysterious. If you are listening to any voice other than your own, you're lost, or, what is more likely, are yet to cross the threshold that marks the beginning: the loss of self-consciousness and, in its place, the detached exploration of self. (1995, p. 7)

A TOPOGRAPHY OF THE UNCONSCIOUS: THE EXTRAORDINARY PRAXIS OF FRANK O'HARA

Martin Flanagan's idea of the necessity for "the loss of self-consciousness" equates well with my notion of the hyperconscious. At first thought it could be said that this state may be achievable by varying means: meditation or sitting in quiet reflection, walking (Wordsworth, Basho), listening to music, climbing hills (Coleridge), taking drugs or alcohol (too many examples of this), dreams (Walwicz, Coleridge, Stevenson), or else it might come through some startling and inexplicable impulse. Whatever the means, I will presume that Valéry's poetic state, or my hyperconscious, is essentially the same among poets in the state of creative impulse, while acknowledging that it will manifest in varying ways and/or degrees of intensity. It might be instructive to look at some individual cases, especially those that may suggest the extreme or the extraordinary, so that we might perceive the range and degree of its topography more concretely.

The known and apparent praxis of Frank O'Hara seems at first examination to suggest an exception to the rule of the waking trance or poetic state, as he is known to have often composed while talking to friends or walking the New York streets. I have chosen O'Hara to examine because of his extraordinary approach to composition, so that we might see that even here, there may be a hyperconscious state identifiable.

As his close friend and fellow-poet Kenneth Koch recalls, O'Hara had the ability "to write a poem when other people were talking, or to even get up in the middle of a conversation, get his typewriter, and write a poem, sometimes participating in the conversation while doing so" (1996, p. 20). What can we make of this for the hyperconscious? Can we say that O'Hara was so relaxed in company or in crowds, his attitude to his poetry was so relaxed, his intentional preparedness so firmly established, that he was easily able to write (engage his hyperconscious) no matter what the circumstances? For O'Hara, perhaps sitting around in cafes or friends' lounge rooms, talking and joking, eating and drinking coffee or wine, was the same for him as Wordsworth's solitary wandering across the hills or Charles Bukowski's drunken solitude in his boarding-house rooms. I have not intended in this discourse to at any stage suggest that the hyperconscious state is always and only indicated by glassy-eyed solitude or trance-like, incommunicable states. Perhaps the common denominator is that it requires some high level of self-knowledge and confidence, no matter what the circumstances, which allows the self to be absent so that the prepared (intentional) poet readily slips into the hyperconscious state. To repeat how Valéry puts it, in Ince's translation and interpretation: "To know oneself really well is... to be on the threshold of original creation" (Ince, 1961, p. 99).

Perhaps it is possible that a poet such as O'Hara, after many years of composing, had such self-knowledge that his access to his creative urge switched on at the least likely times; that the "intention" was so powerfully established that the "unintentional" composition arose without inhibition, without the "existence of the self", when: "In the process of imagining, all the self-regarding data of ordinary life seem to vanish" (Bromwich, 1993, p. 825). It is apparent that O'Hara was a regular drinker, if not an alcoholic, and perhaps it was alcohol that enabled him to move so easily into a hyperconscious state of composition. He was also intent upon a casual approach to his writing that rejected earlier Romantic and post-Romantic models of the poet. Perhaps all of these things contributed to his individual ability.

In his review of O'Hara's *Selected Poems*, Koch remarks in general on the immediacy that is the state of composition and how it expresses the unconscious:

> In catching a feeling in the process of coming into being, or as it first explodes into a thousand refractions, one can hope to reveal some of the truth that lies hidden in our unconscious, in all the things we have known or felt but can't be aware of simultaneously. (1996, p. 25)

This does not suggest that the poet must be secluded (in the garret). Indeed, the verb "catching" suggests that the hunter, the intentional "predator", is waiting to pounce when the prey (mood or impulse) comes; to attack, almost as a cat does a mouse, whence to play with it, as if indifferently, almost unintentionally, so conversant with and in control of its powers is it. The analogy is limited in its application to the poet-hunter but the idea of the "catcher" seems apt. There is a suggestion of alertness, preparedness, and of relaxedness, even passivity, certainly of receptiveness, for the catcher. The catcher knows not when the prey will appear but when it does she or he also knows that she or he will be ready to pounce and in that known, focused state (from experience i.e. praxis), devour it.

It may be possible that O'Hara in fact needed to be among people in order to relax and become unselfconscious, to be "himself"; this was such a common experience for him that it was the only way he could achieve this state. His hyperconsciousness was dependent upon company; it was the busyness of conversation and noise that gave protection to and promotion of his focal state. Much of his work seemed to be written while (and about) being among people, although he also composed while on or after solitary walks around New York streets.

> Able to write while friends were present, he would put a Rachmaninoff piano concerto on the record player, amble over to the typewriter, and bang out a poem. He liked the whole idea of occasional poetry, the idea that poems could be occasioned by circumstance. Anything could qualify as an event. (Lehman, 1998, p. 169)

In his manifesto "Personism", written "in about half an hour" (Lehman, 1998, p. 185), O'Hara declares: "*You just go on your nerve*" (cited in Lehman 1998, p. 185, author's italics). And in an interview with Edward Lucie-Smith, O'Hara said that "the avant-garde always exists in the state of idea" made up with "people who are *bored* by other people's ideas … tired of looking at something that looks like something else" (Lehman, 1998, p. 379, author's italics). Clearly, O'Hara wanted, perhaps needed to write in a way that was not like anyone else. His work was even different in so many ways from his close allies in the New York School of Poetry, Ashbery and Koch, and yet the *idea* was the same: to break the rules, to disrupt the expectations, to refute what his predecessors had done. O'Hara and Ashbery and Koch admired poets like Rimbaud, Apollinaire, Mayakovsky because they too broke with what preceded them, they too were *original*, they too were bored with other people's ideas.

The fact that O'Hara worked this way, in such a spontaneous manner, no matter where he was, in such a "personist" method, "something like a message left on an answering machine" (Lehman, 1998, p. 187) is the reason we can "know" his method, or a great part of it.

In his early, formative years as a poet, the young O'Hara "divided his solitary time between his attic room and the woods and fields near his home" (Gooch, 1993, p. 49). In Brad Gooch's biography of O'Hara, *City Poet: The Life and Times of Frank O'Hara* (1993) there is no clear reference to O'Hara's praxis, but there are allusions to it, indicating that he did work on poems over long periods, even if the lines may have been, at least at the outset, "automatic". "O'Hara worked on 'Second Avenue' (a 478-line poem) mostly in Larry Rivers' plaster garden studio overlooking Second Avenue" (Gooch, 1993, p. 233). The key word here is "mostly" which suggests that O'Hara worked on the poem at various locales, but "mostly" at Rivers' studio, and if he did so, considering the length of the poem, it is possible that he worked on it for some time.

This does not refute the fact that he could and did write while among people, at least in the first instance or draft of the poem, often writing about them and their conversations and movements. So where is the unconscious at work here? In a letter to Rivers, O'Hara wrote: "I do believe that the artist is near the mysteries that govern us or that we govern unconsciously" (Gooch,

1993, p. 233). Like Lysenko and McBryde, perhaps there is some deeper personal drive behind O'Hara's writing on his mundane surroundings. That O'Hara was aware of this is also indicated by Koch: "He [O'Hara] must have felt the power and beauty of unconscious phenomena in surrealist poems, but what he does is to use this power and beauty to ennoble, complicate, and simplify waking actions" (Koch, 1996, p. 25). Indeed, it is O'Hara's need to be and create in this state of imminence that is paramount, not what he wrote about. What it suggests most importantly is the need of the poet to "escape" the overwhelming sense of the self that is always suggesting the future or the past, or time, stealing the life of the moment. In much the same manner, many writers have been noted as composing while seated in cafes and bars: catching the moment and movement of their minds, no matter what the circumstances surrounding them. As Koch suggests:

> he was always thinking, meditating "in an emergency".* It was always in an emergency because one's life had to be experienced and reflected on at the same time, and that is just about impossible. (Koch, 1996, p. 26)

Note that Koch writes "one's life had to be experienced and reflected on at the same time" (1996, p. 26). As already suggested, the hyperconscious state may be the only psychic state where life can be experienced and reflected upon at the same time because the individual is between the experience and the reflection, where "space is disappearing and your singularity" (O'Hara, 1974, p. 103).† In this state the individual can be objectively subjective and subjectively objective (or intentional and unintentional) where exists "the simple dichotomy of self-presence and self-absence" (Earle, 2003, p. 1022). Indeed, the notions of objectivity and subjectivity consume each other. Their

---

* A title of one of O'Hara's books is "Meditations in an Emergency".

† This is a line from O'Hara's poem "Sleeping on the Wing".

complementary opposite-ness* can liberate and ground the individual in the moment of impulsive perception. There is here a suggestion of dynamics, a suggestion that the focal state of the hyperconscious is in flux, whereby the poet can "surface", come in and out of the (deep or shallow) focal intensity, momentarily or for extended periods.

Koch writes: "The speed and accidental aspect of his [O'Hara's] writing are not carelessness but are essential to what the poems are about: the will to catch what is really there and still taking place" (Koch, 1996, p. 25). This could apply equally to the examination of thoughts, such as by Donne or Dickinson et al, as it could to the examination of the mundane, such as by O'Hara or William Carlos Williams. And note again the verb "catch".

O'Hara's poetic did not exclusively deal with the mundane: the "I do this, I do that" poems (Koch, 1996, p. 28). Indeed, he sometimes wrote more abstracted, metaphysical poems, and one such example, "Sleeping on the Wing" could be seen to directly address the idea of the hyperconscious state, not just in its meaning, but in its composition. I want to cite the poem in full and then do a close reading of it in order to investigate the inference that even a poet such as O'Hara recognised the existence and manifestation of the hyperconscious. And yet, it should be pointed out, the poem came about as a result of a challenge to O'Hara's supposed ability to write at will. Gooch quotes James Schuyler:

> 'One Saturday noon I was having coffee with Frank and Joe LeSueur, and Joe and I began to twit him about his ability to write a poem any time, any place,' wrote Schuyler … 'Frank gave us a look – both hot and cold – got up, went into his bedroom and wrote "Sleeping on the Wing", a beauty, in a matter of minutes'. (Gooch, 1993, p. 273)

---

* This is a tenet of eastern philosophy that signifies the essential difference in thinking between east and west: the occidental binaries or dualism and the oriental complimentary oppositeness of things.

Of course the sceptic in me recognises the possibility that the poem already existed in O'Hara's bedroom, written over a period of days or weeks prior to the challenge, but at the same time, given O'Hara's praxis, his finely tuned "intentional preparedness" I can just as easily believe that he did in fact write the poem there and then. But whether it was composed "in a matter of minutes" or not, the fact that he was often witnessed writing poems "in a matter of minutes" suggests the power of poetic intention – the reading, discussing, listening, writing, thinking – had "prepared" O'Hara to do so. But it is the meaning of the poem that I am most interested in here, a meaning that seems to directly address the notion of the hyperconscious.

Even the title, "Sleeping on the Wing", suggests the same paradoxical nature of the hyperconscious, of being "asleep" and awake (flying and observing) at the same time: "life had to be experienced and reflected on at the same time" (Koch, 1996, p. 26). The term "on the wing" is readily interpreted as writing, along the lines of O'Hara's "(going) on your nerve", while "asleep" (unintentional: working from the unconscious), or unconcerned, detached, unselfconscious; asleep to the self, the surrounds, the immediate. It seems that the whole poem could be read metaphorically, as a treatise on the hyperconscious. The lines "soaring above the shoreless city, / veering upward from the pavement" evoke the distancing and objectifying of the sordid world of the city and its people, and might also be interpreted as the escape from self-consciousness, away from the mundane view, the business-like, pedestrian view. Even if that view is still of the mundane, it is not necessarily a mundane view. Appropriately, Koch wrote that what O'Hara did was to: "ennoble, complicate, and simplify waking actions" (Koch, 1996, p. 25).

The enjambment of "as a pigeon / does when a car honks or a door slams" is deliberate, moving *does* to the next line. This suggests that the poet "flies" as a pigeon, as some-thing other than who she or he is. The pigeon is startled by the loud and sudden quotidian noises that limit the view of the seer, the crowded and limited world of doors and other-than-human noises. The poet, like the pigeon is set to fly like a bird from the mundane shocks and limitations, "to avoid some great sadness" into his or her reverie/reflection (poetic state), "the door / of dream ...". This door that slams is the door of the mundane (perhaps even the door of the American Dream?), the idea of which is slammed, "waking" the poet. So that "Once a poet wakes up, he is stupid, I mean intelligent, 'Where am I?' he asks" (Cocteau, 1980, p. 90): the poet sees with the perfect vision of innocence.

What kind of dream is it that O'Hara is referring to, when he writes "of dream, life perpetuated in parti-colored loves / and beautiful lies all in different languages"? O'Hara writes "dream", not "the dream" or "a dream": dream is portrayed as a state of mind, "asleep" to the real, "life perpetuated in parti-colored loves and beautiful lies". All the different languages of New York and the world, this is what the poet "flies" (rhyming with "lies") from. In all the different languages it makes the same "beautiful lies". Note the enjambment here, emphasising the *parti-colored loves / beautiful lies* paring, and the "l" plural words: loves and lies.

Two years later, in 1957, O'Hara wrote, in the poem "In Memory of My Feelings":

> *I rise into the cool skies*
> *and gaze on at the imponderable world with the simple identification*
> (1974, p. 105)

Here O'Hara is more pointedly, less abstractly, alluding to his need and/or act of "flying" above the mundane, imponderable world in order to, perhaps, express it, make some sense of it, cope with it. In the more abstract language of *Sleeping on the Wing* O'Hara writes that with this flight. *Fear drops away too.* This suggests that, as well as "the shoreless city... dream" dropping away, so does the fear: fear of what? Perhaps it is his deep, inescapable fear of the imponderable mundane.

As the line continues with "like the cement, and you", "you and "too" echo each other like "cries", "flies" and "lies".

As well as the cement of your fear, "you" "too" drop away. I see this as your sense of self, your self-consciousness, dropping away. In other words, the fear engendered by self-consciousness: fear of loss, fear of failure, fear of mortality, perhaps even fear of criticism, especially for the artist: the fear of censure and censorship, from one's peers or from the self. Freud's endopsychic defence or censorship can be a result of the fear of being too obvious, too clichéd, too predictable. Only in "flight", from the "self" (a constructed self) can the poet be free to be and see, free to be, to be a seer, so that "*you / are over the Atlantic. Where is Spain? where is / who?*". The delight of the flight is the loss of the need to know anything: the quotidian world is left way behind so which side of the Atlantic you are on is immaterial, until the enemy thought intervenes. In his manifesto, "Personism", O'Hara writes:

> I'm not saying that I don't have practically the most lofty ideas of anyone writing today, but what difference does that make? They're just ideas. The only good thing about it is that when I get lofty enough I've stopped thinking and that's when refreshment arrives. (1974, p. xiii)

When he writes, when he "stops thinking" and "refreshment arrives", O'Hara is lofty as a pigeon flying over the Atlantic. As he writes in the poem, further on: "to be out of, forever, neither in nor for". Further on still, he writes "you are a sculptor dreaming of space / and speed".

But just as the flight is liberating, the thought of where to, where at, where from brings earthly issues to mind. So O'Hara reflects that: "The Civil War was fought to free the slaves, / was it?" O'Hara is being ironic: of course the slaves were freed, but is that what the war was about? And are the slaves freed? Who is "free"? Are the African Americans? Are the Hispanics, the whites? And both Spain and America had their civil wars: to free the slaves, / was it?

What and who is fighting for freedom? The poet "flies" beyond earthly affairs such as these, no matter how historically important they are. But the point is that thought of the world is always there to trap "the sleeper-poet" and bring her or him *back to earth*:

"A sudden down-draught reminds you of gravity / and your position in respect to human love". Consciousness intrudes: the word, "love" again, but not "loves", and here it is "human love" which sounds like a more true concept. And yet, "But/" is on its own, hanging on the end of the line, enjambed for pause, for effect (just as "Dead" is in the final stanza): "But/here [flying/ composing] is where the gods are, speculating, bemused". "Here" where the seer can hear the gods, or be like the gods; where the unselfconscious self can speculate like the gods. Where:

> *Once you are helpless, you are free, can you believe*
> *that? Never to waken to the sad struggle of a face?*
> *to travel always over some impersonal vastness,*
> *to be out of forever, neither in nor for!*

The enjambment of "believe/that" holds us on believe, as in "faith", such a strong force of the worldly "dream". And again, Cocteau reverberates, as well as Eliot's impersonal poet, and Rimbaud's "For *I* is someone else". For only when the poet is "helpless", "free" ("stupid") can she or he be free to "see", *can you believe*, in everything/anything "neither in nor for". The self is obliterated and free to be nowhere, free to express what (who) they are experiencing.

The end of the poem is a celebration of this freedom, this "refreshment", when O'Hara almost declares:

you relinquish ...
the kingdom of your self-sailing ...
as space is disappearing and your singularity

Kafka wrote, "there can never be enough silence around when one writes" (1992, pp. 183–4), and while O'Hara usually wrote when among or near people, he could create this "silence" when and because even space was disappearing "and your singularity", because without the self conscious of the self there is no spatial existence.

THIS OTHER WHO FLIES: THROUGH LACAN, THE POEM IS THE ALIBI

From the above, the question arises: just who is speaking or escaping the self when using the language of the lyric poem? Lacan addresses this question when he asks not just who is speaking but who (or what) is being spoken "about" or through? This question is crucial to understanding what "frees" the poet to create (to fly) from what mostly inhibits them (O'Hara's "cement"/"pavement"); not just their sense of themselves, but their sense of who it is that is "represented" in the poem and what the language *means* to others. Lacan addresses this question thus: "It is not a question of knowing whether I speak of myself in a way that conforms to what I am, but rather a knowing whether I am the same as that of which I speak." (Lacan, 2004, p. 456). The key word here is "conform" because Lacan recognises the impossibility of a defined self, a prefigured self which, when attributed, immediately places a gap between the self and the self's perception as the self. This seems to be what O'Hara is referring to as his "disappearing ... singularity" (1974, p. 103). Lacan expresses this as a question: "Is the place that I occupy as the subject of a signifier concentric or excentric, in relation to the place I occupy as subject of the signified?" (Lacan, 2004, p. 456). In other words: does the perspective on the subject of the self begin or come from the observing self (concentric) or does it begin or come from the observed self (excentric)? Does the subject of the signifier (poet) begin from a point of "knowing" who he or she is and circle in on that knowledge (conform/concentric), or do they begin with no knowledge and explore outward, excentrically, "knowing" only that they (signifier/poet) are the "same as that of which [signified] I speak" (not-conforming/excentric)? In order to address the conundrum of the disappearing singularity this may be put more simply as: is the poet the same person as that of whom they speak?

This question is, for Lacan, central to defining "the topography of the unconscious" as defined by the Saussurean algorithm, and explored by Lacan as:

> This signifying game between metonymy and metaphor, up to and including the active edge that splits my desire between a refusal of the signifier [the signifying chain] and a lack of being. (2004, p. 457)

In his examination of this conundrum Lacan eventually concludes that:

> That is to say, what is needed is more than these words with which, for a brief moment I disconcerted my audience: I think where I am not, therefore I am where I do not think. Words that render sensible to an ear properly attuned with what elusive ambiguity the ring of meaning flees from our grasp along the verbal thread.
>
> What one ought to say is: I am not wherever I am the plaything of my thought, I think of what I am where I do not think to think. (2004, p. 457)

Of course Lacan is talking of the condition of subjectivity itself here, but he goes on to say that "[t]his two-sided mystery is linked to the fact that the truth can be evoked only in that dimension of alibi in which 'realism' in creative works takes its virtue from metonymy" (2004, p. 457). Accordingly, the poet is, in the act of creative work, already where she or he does not think to think; and when they can likewise accede "to meaning only through the double twist of metaphor when we have the one and only key: the S and the s of the Saussurian algorithm... which is nowhere" (2004, p. 457). The poet needs to not think, in order to think; only then will they be who they are, and then the poem will be "true". As O'Hara says in his Personism manifesto: "when I get lofty enough I've stopped thinking and that's when refreshment arrives" (O'Hara, 1974, p. xiii). Of course there is clearly much irony in O'Hara's manifesto, but there are also serious ideas behind the humour.

This dimension of alibi Lacan alludes to can be applied to the poet's "absence" with the excuse or alibi that they are where they do not think to think, or that they are in a state of mind (hyperconsciousness) where in order to think "clearly" and hence to express that clarity of their unconscious selves (and not their conscious selves) enough to express as much as is possible their true selves in language, a language that nevertheless is part of and not part of themselves. The poem is the alibi: it says: "I (the poet) am not here", but paradoxically, it is the poet, "unintentionally" speaking through the poem.

It is important to keep in mind that although Lacan and Freud often made reference to poetry and language, they were essentially explicating psychoanalysis, and here I am attempting to draw their ideas on the unconscious from psychoanalysis into the examination of the psyche of the poet in the act of composition. The work of Lacan I have been examining was recorded in 1957, and it may be useful for the understanding of the role of the unconscious in poetry composition to examine, finally, his thoughts on the unconscious twenty years later, in his lecture, *Subversion of the subject and dialectic of desire.* In this lecture Lacan suggests: "the right way to reply to the question, 'Who is speaking?', when it is the subject of the unconscious that is at issue. For this reply cannot come from the subject if he does not know what he is saying, or even if he is speaking, as the entire experience of analysis has taught us" (Lacan, 1989, p. 299).

In other words, the subject cannot say who is speaking (or what or even if they are speaking) if what they are saying is coming from the unconscious. Similarly, the poet cannot say who is writing when they do not know what they are writing, or that they are writing, if they are writing mostly from their unconscious: this is what I am arguing for the hyperconscious. If it is the unconscious speaking (writing), the poet does not know why they are speaking (writing), and thus they do not know what they are saying (writing). But who is the poet? Of course, the poet, even in a heightened state of focus or hyperconsciousness will be aware that they are writing, but what they are saying, or why exactly, they cannot be certain of, even if they think that they are certain, as with the extreme examples of Lysenko and McBryde. In order to avoid any spuriousness it should be pointed out that any form of certainty could be seen as dubious. It is true that many poets believe that they know what they are saying (and this may, in part, be true) but it is arguable, if not always provable, that they do not.

In John Muller and William Richardson's analysis of Lacan, they address this section of the 1977 lecture thus:

> This unconscious is both immanent and transcendent to individual subjects, and marks the frontier beyond which the traditional subject, presumed to be "transparent" to himself, loses the self-transparency and begins to "fade", with all the consequent effects that lead to those characteristic manifestations of unconscious process, such as slips of the tongue, witticisms, etc. (Muller & Richardson, 1982, p. 359)

One could readily indicate the manifestations of this "etc" as: distortion, condensation, displacement, overdetermination: metaphor and metonymy. Muller and Richardson are making clear the link between Lacan's finding that "the truth can be evoked only in that dimension of alibi in which all 'realism' in created works takes its virtue from metonymy" (Lacan, 2004, p. 457) and the unconscious stuff of lyric poetry that I am indicating as paralleled in Freud's notion of dream content.*

Muller and Richardson continue:

> In more technical terms, what happens here is that the "cut" *(coupure)* in the discourse, i.e., the bar between the signifier and signified – a fundamental principle of linguistics and basic ingredient of the law of language – begins to have its effect. The result is that the irruptions of unconscious processes into conscious discourse become more manifest – and these are the focus of psychoanalysis. (Muller & Richardson, 1982, p. 359)

For the purposes of this study, these irruptions of unconscious processes into conscious discourse are what define the hyperconscious: the irruptions drive the substance of the lyric poem.

RIMBAUD'S "FOR I IS SOMEONE ELSE"

According to Lacan,

> The end that Freud's discovery proposes for man was defined by him [as] ... : *Wo es war, soll Ich warden* ... [which] means "Where the unconscious was, consciousness shall go". I must come to the place where that was.
> This is one of reintegration and harmony, I could even say of reconciliation (*Versohnung*). (2004, p. 460)

It could equally be said that the poet, in delving into the unconscious, is also "after" reintegration and harmony, even reconciliation, as they feel

* I say dream content because I am not convinced that the dream thoughts can ever be confidently asserted as a true interpretation. But this is not crucial to this discussion, so I will not pursue it further.

the disintegration and disharmony in their self so fiercely; feel the need to reconcile the self, whether consciously or not. As Rimbaud put it so well: "For *I* is someone else (*Car je est un autre*) ... The first study of the man who wants to be a poet is the knowledge of himself, complete. He looks for his soul, inspects it, tests it, learns it." (Rimbaud, 1996, p. 305). The lyric poet may have a greater need of self-knowledge, and has this need because they have too great a sense of themselves, for whatever reason, and this is what drives them to investigate, to understand, to reconcile, to express or "explain" themselves to themselves. It bears repeating that this drive is mostly unconscious: the poet may be aware of the feeling of the drive but not necessarily what it is; not aware of the extent of the deep, subterranean and unconscious self seeking the self.

How the poet approaches this search will vary of course, but it is worthy of further conjecture. Rimbaud had an interesting and famous view on it. He continued his letter to Demeny, stipulating the poet's path to "complete" "knowledge of himself" thus:

> But the soul must be made monstrous... I say one must be a *seer*, make oneself a *seer*.
>
> The poet makes himself a *seer* by a long, gigantic and rational *derangement* of *all the senses*. All forms of love, suffering, and madness. He searches himself. He exhausts all poisons in himself and keeps only their quintessences ... Because he reaches the *unknown*! Since he cultivated his soul, rich already, more than any man! He reaches the unknown, and when, bewildered, he ends by losing the intelligence of his visions, he has seen them. (1966, p. 307)

This is the young Rimbaud, aged 17, declaring in his extreme agonism the necessity to reach that height that, for him, has not been reached by anyone since the Greeks except Racine and Baudelaire. For Rimbaud, the poet must become a seer through the "derangement of his senses", so that he or she can "feel" the need to reconcile; to become lost so that she or he might discover "home" more readily (are there resonances of *The Odyssey* here?). They feel the need to experience existence, emotionally and psychologically, *in extremis* (or because they feel it intensely), and subsequently to reconcile it. In order to find themself the poets first must become lost so that "when ... he ends by losing the intelligence of his visions, he has seen them" (1966, p. 307).

Wallace Fowlie, in his *Critical Study of Rimbaud*, paraphrases and explicates Rimbaud, suggesting the notion of the unselfconscious or detached exploration of self, where the poet might experience the deeper, truer, unknown, unconscious self:

> There are two selves in the poet, a deeply hidden, mysterious self who in the act of poetry destroys the familiar self of the controlled and predictable responses. What Rimbaud terms *voyance* is the vision of the unknown, hidden self. It is one way or one method of contemplating the absolute. Rimbaud speaks of having recently watched this new kind of thought rise to the surface of his consciousness, of having been present at the birth of his thought. (Fowlie, 1965, p. 97)

This seems akin to the unconscious rising to consciousness and fits in well with what I am suggesting in this study. The need for the poet's "derangement", according to Rimbaud (and Fowlie), is for them to be "lost" to their usual way of thinking, their usual language, to experience existence and at the same time be *absent*, unselfconscious, which also seems to parallel this study and Lacan's ... Perhaps if we take the word derangement more broadly (I am not necessarily suggesting that Rimbaud meant it this way) we might see that it could allude to the loss of the knowledge of the self, the loss of self-consciousness. Fowlie elaborates on this attitude of Rimbaud:

> Of the two ways of knowledge, intellectual progress and self-knowledge, Rimbaud advocates the second ... The goal of such self-

> exploration is the unknown ... The supreme language that Rimbaud has in mind, is not the means of knowing, but of forgetting ordinary language, a means of losing one's self and of discovering one's monstrous nature. (1965, p. 98–9)

Fowlie makes a reference to Rolland de Renéville's study of Rimbaud, where he "considered these poetic experiments comparable to the exercises of the Hindu mystics by which they try to merge their will with the universal consciousness" (1965, p. 99). But poets such as Rimbaud are looking to this mystical state so that they may express it in a "supreme language", and to do so while maintaining the not-maintaining of the not-self. Perhaps Lysenko and McBryde were, at least in the two poems examined, doing this: unconsciously hiding their "monstrous nature", or what they, or their unconscious guilt and anger (respectively), were aware of.

The extreme that Rimbaud suggested and felt represents the need for the individual to sink into themselves in such a way as to lose themselves (derange) in order to discover the "uncovered" or quintessential self. The word "derange" comes from the Old French (C18) *desrengier*, literally "move from orderly rows" (Concise Oxford, 2004): hence, move from the orderly rows of the mind. Of course, the extent or mode of "movement" for each poet will be different and more or less extreme, and this extremity will not necessarily indicate the poetic level achieved. I am citing Rimbaud's ideas in order to support my notion of the need for the poets to lose themselves in order to reveal themselves, to "move the orderly rows" or to move what is normal for the psyche. Fowlie's appraisal of Rimbaud's extreme position points to the extreme lengths Rimbaud envisioned and undertook. He speaks of the "stifling of one's self" but he is not, I believe (and nor am I), suggesting that this extreme position of Rimbaud is necessary for the high achievement of the lyric:

> To demand what Rimbaud did of poetry and of another being is to make a pact with Satan or at least with a force representing such a delirious goal that one ceases thereby to be completely human ... To know, as Rimbaud wanted to know, is equivalent to denying one's self ... It is equivalent to a stifling of one's self and the gradual demonization or *abrutissement* he went through. He learned thereby to live in primitive, unconscious zones of his body, but he was never able to leave his body or change his body as he had hoped. He had, finally, to accept man's condition of being. (Fowlie, 1965, p. 229)

It is arguable that Rimbaud, by his extreme attempts to express his need, to articulate his manifesto, only contributed to his lack of unselfconsciousness, only aided his loss of that *quintessence* that had, perhaps more easily, more naturally possessed him in his youth. This is the tragedy and the triumph of Rimbaud: that he needed to state his manifesto in order to impress (on) Demeny (and Izambard, to whom he wrote a similar, though less impassioned and less detailed letter two days earlier) because he feared the compromise of his acquired knowledge as a result of his economic circumstances. He was dependent on his mother, who wanted him to work. His letter to Demeny of 28 August 1871 spells this out clearly. The poems of this time and those prior to 1871 seem the purest, simplest, most beautifully achieved and effective; the most unselfconscious, or hyperconscious. I am referring to poems such as "The First Evening", "At the Cabaret-Vert" and "The Sly Girl". After this, there is no doubting the development and sophistication in his language and of his metaphysical themes along the lines of his letter-manifesto. But this is the problem: after 1871 the poems become increasingly self-conscious, reflexive, and intellectual, and arguably less affecting, at least to this reader. Is it possible that he is referring to this in his much admired "Season in Hell" with the opening lines?

> *Long ago, if my memory serves me, my life was a banquet where everyone's heart was generous, and where all wines flowed.*

One evening I pulled Beauty down on my knees. I found her embittered and I cursed her.
I took arms against injustice.
I ran away. O witches, poverty, hate – I have confided my treasure to you!

And, some eight lines further on in the poem he reflects:

But recently, on the verge of giving my last croak, I thought of looking for the key to the ancient banquet where I might possibly recover my appetite. (Rimbaud, 1966, p. 173)

Is it conceivable that Rimbaud is alluding to his "lost" lostness, that state that initially, in his teens, enabled him to write with such "Beauty", at the banquet of nature when "all wines flowed"? And has he now lost this state because he has "confided (his) treasure" to the "witches, poverty, hate"? Is it that having spoken, and thus objectified the treasures, playing "clever tricks on insanity" (lines 12, 13), he has now bought about his loss of innocence, his loss of aesthetic?

Perhaps, despite the reflexive nature of the later work, this nevertheless makes these works his greater works after all, as they reveal more profoundly his erring and regret, and because of their allusions to poetry and the psychology of composition. But this question of merit or regression is not the central concern of this dissertation. This small survey of Rimbaud is intended to add to the discussion on the power of the unconscious in the hyperconscious act. Rimbaud is relevant because of the extreme position he took: he represents a blatant example, in his rapid and short development, of what I am proposing. His early recognition at such a young age (although this recognition is not as great as the attention and fame he received after he left France and certainly not as great as after he died), perhaps contributed to his loss of innocence – his loss of loss of self – and perhaps helped make him increasingly arrogant and hostile, until he eventually abandoned poetry altogether; not because of Verlaine and his other peers, but because of poetry, because it had abandoned him.

Rimbaud advocates the means to self-knowledge exclusively through "love, suffering, madness". The point is that, while these states, vague as they are, indicate an unselfconsciousness (lost and transcendent), the history of poetry would indicate that they are not the "exclusive" means to the hyperconscious, not the only gateway. Indeed, while these states of "love, suffering, madness" are mostly those of the juvenile or "young" poets who died relatively young (Rimbaud, Keats, Plath, Dransfield), they might indeed indicate that if the poet can survive such ravages they might achieve the hyperconscious state through a highly developed or even a natural experience of detached (unselfconscious) exploration of self. On the other hand, there may be more serene avenues to the hyperconscious. There are no doubt all manner of means, but the major point remains that all of them seem to involve a need to escape the sense of self in the act of writing, whether by suffering, or through joy, or via detached calm.

In this state of unselfconscious focus, or hyperconsciousness, which evolves from being a poet and writing poetry (intention and unintention), the unconscious can freely operate without prompting or expectation. Of course there are available inducements such as drugs or alcohol, and although it must be conceded that many poets and artists throughout history have used such substances, especially in their youth, they have done so at their cost – often an ultimate cost – or else these substances have been ultimately counter-productive. But this is an area of argument outside the province of this dissertation. The sense of unselfconscious freedom that I am suggesting, like all freedoms, is a battle to sustain in any society, but that it exists in varying degrees and forms seems undeniable.

CONCLUSION

In this dissertation I have aimed to establish some understanding of the creative process as distinct from the analytical process in the writing of lyric poetry, identifying three basic stages in the process: 1. Intention. 2. Unintention. 3. Review. I have explored the notion of intention or preparedness or vocation in some detail, but I have focused on the second stage of unintention, the immediate moment of initial impulse, arguing that it is here we might find the most evidence of what it is that drives the poet to write, and what form or language that writing might take. I have developed a historical examination of the "poetic state" in order to establish and identify an idea of the psyche of the lyric poet in the time of creative impulse, and I have named this state as the hyperconscious. I have not clearly defined this state but I have indicated, by examining the work of Freud and Lacan, that its drives are akin to those psychological states of dreams, where the unconscious is driving the psyche. This has led to an examination of what I call the *poet-paradox,* whereby the poet becomes so absorbed in the poem that they cease to think of themselves as themselves in order to write, without self-consciousness.

I have focused mostly on three distinct poems by three separate poets as case studies, and all three poems and poets are extremes, chosen in order to show the extreme that establishes a possible truth: Lysenko's "Chimney", and McBryde's "Last Fathom" have similar origins or drives, extreme evidence of the unconscious or "unintention"; O'Hara's extremeness is his apparent lack of a poetic state, which, I argue, is merely a less apparent poetic state that he has learned. This is the culmination of his intention. I have cited and unpacked his poem "Sleeping on the Wing" as a kind of poetic essay describing his need for this poetic state; a poem, ironically, that he wrote after being challenged by poet-friends that he could not compose a poem spontaneously.

In the creative act of first instance for the lyric poet, the unconscious emerges in concert with other parts of the psyche in the form of the hyperconscious or unintention of the poet, prepared as they are to act through a vocational intention. Given that the unconscious cannot be axiomatically established, we nevertheless might through this study gain some new insight into it and the hyperconscious; whereby the lyric poet might increase their understanding of the process that they are undertaking or have undertaken towards: "the knowledge of himself, complete" (Rimbaud, 1966, p. 307).

APPENDIX: "LAST FATHOM" BY IAN MCBRYDE

FROM *EQUATORIAL*, FIVE ISLANDS PRESS, WOLLONGONG, 2001 (PP. 103–5)

Based upon the events of Monday August 5, 1987, when Australian submarine HMAS Otama dived ten nautical miles south-east of Sydney, leaving on the surface two sailors who had been working in the conning tower. The bodies of Seaman Damien Humphreys, 19, and Able Seaman Hugh Markcroiu, 24, were never recovered.

1040

The first stab of panic
comes with the wet roar
of air escaping
from the ballast tanks
and the impossible sensation

of descent. Both of us
banging our wrenches
on the deaf metal, shouting
above the shudder and grind

of engines and then
the black pacific slap
of water.

1041

The kid's face
whitening with alarm
as the hull's shoulder
falls away beneath our feet.

I can't breathe!

Relax. Move your arms
kick your feet, keep
your head back.

Crow I can't!

Watch me. Move your arms
slowly, back and forth
under the surface, like this.

1059

Kick your feet, like you're walking
in the water. Remember,
at the academy,
remember?

Relax. Watch me.
Good.

1127

Crow I'm
walking I'm walking
in the water,
like you said.

Good. Keep walking.
I close my eyes, try
to lie on my back.
My neck unstretches.

1245

Crow, tell her.

It seems much later.
All is salt.
The water is
softening me.

Crow.

1310

The kid vomits.
Half-digested strands

of tomato jerk past
on the vertical surface.

His hands flutter, striving
to push the wave away.

1422

The ocean is choking me.
I wonder what
she's doing now,
what she's wearing,
who she's with.

1538

Crow tell her.
Tell my mother.

My stiff fingers find his,
grip hard. He feels blue.
Hold on to me.

Don't think, just
stop him, prop him
up, don't think just
keep him from sinking.

1712

Getting dark.
His slack lips silver
in the fading light.
The mechanical chatter
of his teeth as he
rides die sea with me.

Crow I never

It's alright.
It doesn't matter.

I always liked her
in that yellow dress.

1757

Suddenly up above,
helicopters, their lights
seen dimly through
the rain, the weight
of sound flattening us
into sudden troughs.

He lets go
of my hand to wave,
his head back,
his throat open.

Searchlights to either side
of us, both of us
screaming and screaming
as the aircraft
circle and move on.

1801

They saw us,
they saw us
didn't they Crow?

A massive surge of swell
and his distant voice
from the other side
of the wave.
Crow come
back come

1824

I forgive everyone.
I wish I'd kissed
her goodbye.

Thought I heard
the kid's voice
but it couldn't be him.

1853

Salt.

Frozen.

Someone will come.

The yellow dress.

Yes. I can hold on.

I can stay afloat until

someone comes.

BIBLIOGRAPHY

Adorno, T.W., 1991–1992, "On lyric poetry and society", *Notes to literature,* Vol. 1, R. Tiedemann ed., S.W. Nicholsen (trans.), Columbia University Press, New York.

Baudelaire, C., 1969, "The salon of 1846", *Romanticism,* JB Halsted ed., Macmillan, London.

Berrigan, T., 1997, "Incredible masterpieces", *On the level everyday: Selected talks on poetry and the art of living,* J., Lewis ed., Talisman House, New Jersey.

Bromwich, D., 1993, "Negative capability", *The new Princeton encyclopedia of poetry and Poetics,* A. Preminger & T.V.F. Brogan eds., Princeton University Press, New Jersey.

Brophy, K., 1998, *Creativity,* University of Melbourne Press, Melbourne.

Clark, T., 1997, *The theory of inspiration,* Manchester University Press, Manchester.

Cocteau, J., 1980, *Opium – The diary of a cure,* Grove Press, New York.

De Quincey, T., 1961, *Reminiscences of the English lake poets,* revised edn., J.M. Dent & Sons, London.

Eagleton, T., 1996, *The illusions of postmodernism,* Blackwell, Oxford.

Earle, B., 2003, "Tarrying with the negative: Baudelaire, Mallarmé, and the rhythm of modernity", *Modern Language Notes,* Vol. 118, No. 4., pp. 1015–42.

Eliot, T.S., 1965, "Tradition and the individual talent" 1919, *Selected prose,* edn., J. Hayward ed., Penguin, London, pp. 21–30.

Ferguson, SC 1988, "Defining the short story (impressionism and form)" in *Essentials of the theory of fiction* (2nd edn.), MJ Hoffman & PD Murphy eds., Duke University Press, Durham, pp. 287–300.

Flanagan, M., 1995, "A good critic must be a good writer first", *The Age* Melbourne, 5 August.

Forbes, J., 1993, "Interview with Cath Kenneally", *Otus Rush*, no. 8, pp. 88–102.

Forbes, J., 1998, *Collected poems*, Brandl & Schlesinger, Sydney.

Fowlie, W., 1965, *Rimbaud: A critical study*, University of Chicago Press, Chicago.

Freud, S., 2004, "The interpretation of dreams", *Literary theory: An anthology*, 2nd edn., J. Rivkin & M. Ryan eds., Blackwell Publishing, Malden, MA, pp. 397–413.

Freud, S., 1908, "Creative writers and day-dreaming", *Standard Edition*, Vol. 9.

Freud, S., 1985, "Humour", *The pelican Freud library*, Vol. 14, *Art and Literature*, Penguin, UK.

Freud, S., 2001 "The Uncanny", *The Norton Anthology of Theory and Criticism*, W.W. Norton & Co., New York.

Gooch, B., 1993, *City poet: The life and times of Frank O'Hara*, Knopf, New York.

Hemingway, E., 1999, *Death in the afternoon* (First Scribner Classic edn.), Scribner Classics, New York.

Ince, W.N., 1961, *The poetic theory of Paul Valéry (inspiration and technique)*, Leicester University Press, Leicester.

Jung, C.G., 1952, "Psychology and literature", *The Creative Process*, translated by W.S. Dell and Cary F. Baynes, The New American Library, University of California (1933).

Kafka, F., 1992, *Letters to Felice / Franz Kafka* [edn.], J. Stern & E. Duckworth (trans.), Minerva, London.

Keats, J., 1952, *The letters of John Keats*, 4th edn., MB Forman ed., Oxford University Press, London.

Koch, K., 1996, *The art of poetry (poems, parodies, interviews, essays, and other work)*, University of Michigan Press, Ann Arbor.

Kristeva, J., 2002, "Revolution in poetic language", *The portable Kristeva*, K Oliver ed., Columbia University Press, New York.

Lacan, J., 1989, *Écrits, a selection* (3rd reprint), A. Sheridan (trans.), Tavistock/ Routledge, London.

Lacan, J., 2004, "The instance of the letter in the unconscious or reason since Freud",

Literary theory: An anthology, Blackwell, Malden, MA, pp. 447–61.

Langbaum, R., 1978, *The word from below (essays on modern literature and culture)*, University of Wisconsin Press, Wisconsin.

Lehman, D., 1998, *The last avant-garde*, Doubleday, New York.

Lewis, D.O. & Lewis, M., 1976, "The psychoanalytic model of a dream used as poetic", *Psychoanalytic Review*, Vol. 63.

Lysenko, M., 1998, *Winning and losing*, Hit & Miss Publishers, Melbourne.

McBryde, I., 2001, *Equatorial*, Five Islands Press, Wollongong.

McCooey, D., 2005, "Surviving Australian poetry: The new lyricism" *Blue Dog*, Vol. 4, No.7, pp. 62–70.

Muller, J.P. & Richardson W.J., 1982, *Lacan and language, a reader's guide to Écrits*, International Universities Press, New York.

Murray, L., "Interview with Les Murray", 1998, *Desert Island Disks*, radio broadcast, BBC Radio 4 (transcription provided by Peter Alexander). *Writing Poetry*, http://www.lesmurray.org/writingpoetry.htm.

O'Hara, F., 1974, *The Selected poems of Frank O'Hara*, D. Allen ed., Vintage Books, New York, pp. 102–3.

Rickword, E., 1971, *Rimbaud: The boy and the poet*, Haskell House, New York.

Rimbaud, A., 1966, *Rimbaud, complete works, selected letters*, W. Fowlie (trans.), University of Chicago Press, Chicago.

Rose, D., 2006, *Consciousness (philosophical, psychological and neural theories)*, Oxford University Press, Oxford.

Shklovsky, V., 1965, "Art as technique", *Russian formalist criticism: Four essays*, L.T. Lemon & M.J. Reis (trans.), University of Nebraska Press, Lincoln.

Shklovsky, V., 1973, "The resurrection of the word (1914)", *Russian Formalism*, S. Bann & J.E. Bowlt eds., R. Sherwood (trans.),* Scottish Academy Press, Edinburgh.

Shklovsky, V., 1977, "Introduction" by Richard Sheldon, *Third Factory*, Ardis, Ann Arbor, pp. vii–xxx.

* This may be an error in the book: it possibly should be Richard Sheldon.

Valéry, P., 1953, *La Jeune Parque*, Gallimard, Paris.

Valéry, P., 1958, *The art of poetry*, D. Folliot (trans.), Routledge & Kegan Paul, London.

Williams, C.K., 1998, *Poetry and consciousness*, University of Michigan Press, Ann Arbor.

Wimsatt Jr., William K. and Beardsley, Monroe C., 1954 "The Intentional Fallacy", *Verbal Icon: Studies in the Meaning of Poetry*, University of Kentucky Press, Kentucky.

Wimsatt Jr., William K. and Beardsley, Monroe C., 2001, "The Intentional Fallacy", *The Norton Anthology of Theory and Criticism,* W.W. Norton & Co., New York.

Winnicott, D.W. 1965, *The maturational process and the facilitating environment (studies in the theory of emotional development)*, The Hogarth Press, London.

Wordsworth, W. 1974, *The Prose Works of William Wordsworth*, Vol. II, W.J.B. Owen & J.W. Smyser eds., Oxford University Press, London.

Wordsworth, W. 1986, "Lyric Ballads" (Preface), *The Norton Anthology of English Literature*, Vol. 2, ed. A.M. Abrams, W.W. Norton & Co., New York.

Printed in Australia
AUHW020835261121
356052AU00004B/5

9 781925 588804